MW00439215

A PLUME BOOK

SEX AND THE KITTY

NANCY THE CAT is a familiar furry face in homes and businesses around Harpenden, England. She lives with her owner, Melissa Tredinnick, Melissa's husband and their children, and the family's noncelebrity cat, Pip.

a celebrity  *meowmoir*

Sex
and the
Kitty

Nancy the Cat

A PLUME BOOK

PLUME
Published by Penguin Group
Penguin Group (USA) Inc., 375 Hudson Street, New York, New York 10014, U.S.A. •
Penguin Group (Canada), 90 Eglinton Avenue East, Suite 700, Toronto, Ontario, Canada
M4P 2Y3 (a division of Pearson Penguin Canada Inc.) • Penguin Books Ltd., 80 Strand,
London WC2R 0RL, England • Penguin Ireland, 25 St. Stephen's Green, Dublin 2, Ireland
(a division of Penguin Books Ltd.) • Penguin Group (Australia), 250 Camberwell Road,
Camberwell, Victoria 3124, Australia (a division of Pearson Australia Group Pty. Ltd.) •
Penguin Books India Pvt. Ltd., 11 Community Centre, Panchsheel Park, New Delhi – 110
017, India • Penguin Books (NZ), 67 Apollo Drive, Rosedale, Auckland 0632, New Zealand
(a division of Pearson New Zealand Ltd.) • Penguin Books (South Africa) (Pty.) Ltd., 24
Sturdee Avenue, Rosebank, Johannesburg 2196, South Africa

Penguin Books Ltd., Registered Offices: 80 Strand, London WC2R 0RL, England

First published by Plume, a member of Penguin Group (USA) Inc.

First Printing, September 2011
10 9 8 7 6 5 4 3 2 1

 REGISTERED TRADEMARK—MARCA REGISTRADA

LIBRARY OF CONGRESS CATALOGING-IN-PUBLICATION DATA

Tredinnick, Melissa.
   Sex and the kitty : a celebrity meowmoir / Nancy the Cat.
      p.   cm.
   ISBN 978-0-452-29742-5
   1. Cats—Fiction.   2. Celebrities—Fiction.   3. Cats—Humor.   4. Satire.
I. Title.   II. Title: Celebrity meowmoir.
   PS3620.R4415S49   2011
   813'.6—dc22

                                                        2011022735

Printed in the United States of America
Set in Goudy Old Style
Designed by Eve L. Kirch

For Phil. We couldn't have done it without you.

Contents

Introduction

I did encounter some skepticism when I announced that I intended to write my memoirs. "But Nancy, you're not even two years old!" people cried, as if a cat could not possibly have achieved enough in such a short time to merit an autobiography. Granted, I am on the young side to release a memoir. Most cats don't have their biographies published until they are the wrong side of middle age (or even until they have popped their proverbial clogs). But I have never been one to follow the path set by other cats.

I prefer to take my inspiration from human celebrities—such icons as Charlotte Church, Justin Bieber, and the Kardashian sisters. A cynic might say they were also too young for an autobiography, and yet look how many books they've sold. Wisdom has nothing to do with age, as I'm sure the Misses Kardashian would agree. Plus, I am not stupid. By getting my first memoir out now, I am leaving the door open for possible sequels.

They say that once you become famous you stay the same age in the public consciousness forever, and that certainly seems to be the case with me. I first gained notoriety as a kitten, which, combined with the fact that I am naturally petite (size 0, for the record), means that in the public's mind I am synonymous with youth. You could say I'm the Donny Osmond of the cat world. But I digress.

Before we start, I'd like to get a few things straight. I can't bear people who complain that a book "wasn't what they were expecting," as if an author's work was answerable to a reader's ill-informed expectations. So to spare the critics among you the dull ache of disappointment, I'm going to set out a few ground rules. That way you will all know what you're letting yourselves in for.

🐾 Contrary to the prevailing trend in the autobiography genre, this is not a misery memoir. Without wanting to spoil the ending, no one dies. I didn't overcome a tragic infancy or survive abuse and neglect. I'm not deaf, blind, an amputee, or in any other way "special." I'm just an ordinary cat.

🐾 Nor will this be an uplifting story of the power of cats to change the world. I have never saved anyone's life, human or feline. I haven't healed a community or taught my owner the meaning of true love. I will leave such worthy endeavors to the (many) other cats who have tapped that particular literary vein.

🐾 I also have a zero-tolerance policy toward cat-based puns.* If you're looking for a "hiss-and-tell" memoir or hoping this book will be "bursting with *cat*itude," then return this volume to the shelf and step away from the pet biogra-

---

* The sharp-eyed among you may have noticed that there is in fact a cat pun in the title of my book. You can blame my editor for this. She thought it would help sales.

phy section. I'm the first to admit that there is humor to be found in a good bit of feline wordplay, but there is a time and a place for it, and that is on the Internet, probably underneath a photo of a kitten pulling a stupid face.

🐾 Wherever possible, I have used real names. If any of the cats featured in these pages has a problem with that—well, too bad. You're a cat. I'm a cat. What are you going to do, sue me?

My memoir is an account of the first year (and a bit) of my life, the journey I went on in my quest for fame, and the cats I encountered along the way. It is written with both human and feline readers in mind. Whether you're a cat, a cat owner, or even one of those alarming women who collects cats and wears cat-themed clothing, there's something in here for you. Of course I will be delighted if *Cat* magazine selects my memoir as its book of the month, but I also have my sights set on Oprah's Book Club. I could make myself quite at home on that sofa of hers, thank you very much.

Finally, just for the record, I am writing this book myself. Aficionados of the genre will appreciate how unusual this is. Look closely at the covers of most feline memoirs and you will see a human's name lurking underneath the cat's name. Not on my cover. I can guarantee that no human ghostwriters were harmed in the making of this memoir. I was offered one: my agent thought it might help me to "find my voice." But she soon learned, as will you, that finding my voice has never been a problem.

So relax. Have a wash (if you're a cat), make yourself a cup of tea (if you're a human), or clear yourself a space on the sofa (if you're a crazy cat woman) and let me tell you a little bit about myself. I'm going to start at the beginning, so those of you who only bought this book because it mentions sex in the title will need to be patient. There will be plenty to get your heart racing—I promise.

Sex and the Kitty

CHAPTER 1

Home

*A journey of a thousand miles must begin
with a single step.*

—Lao-tzu

I don't remember much about the house I was born in, or indeed about my mother, as I only spent two months of my life
with her and for the first ten days of that I couldn't open my eyes.
But don't go feeling sorry for me—like I said, this isn't a misery
memoir. That's just the way things work in the cat world. I remember other adult cats living in the house, too, as well as an
Alsatian dog with a bloodcurdling bark that belied his puppyish
disposition. My siblings and I were confined to the kitchen,
which contained our food, a cardboard box that served as our
collective bed, and a litter tray. I was aware of my mother and the
other adult cats coming and going through a cat flap in the back
door, but at such a tender age it didn't cross my mind to wonder
what lay beyond. The four walls of that kitchen contained my
world, and I was happy to spend my days playing with my siblings and cuddling up with my mother to sleep.

Like all her offspring, my mother was a black shorthair. She
was also something of a tearaway, and as we drifted off to sleep
at night, she would tell how she had managed to open a locked
window in order to answer the call of nature (or at least, the call

of a neighborhood tom) and get pregnant with us. I dare say the Freudians among you are having a field day right now, speculating about whether my subsequent daredevil behavior can be attributed to my mother's example. You may well be right. By human standards, all cats should be basket cases: most of us never knew our fathers and were forcibly separated from our mothers in infancy. If we were human we could keep the self-help industry in business for life. But alley cats such as myself tend to be emotionally robust and optimistic by nature; our milk bowl is half full, rather than half empty. (Pedigree cats are another matter, but I'll come to them later.)

We may not have had long together, but in our brief time as a family unit my mother taught me a vital life lesson: black cats are not rated highly in the cute-stakes.* You might have noticed how cat shelters are always full of black cats. More often than not it is black kittens who are left on the special-offers shelf in the supermarket of life, valued at half the price of their tabby, marmalade, and calico peers. So it was with me and my siblings, and my mother's owner was unable to find anyone to home us until, in desperation, she enlisted the help of a cat charity.

Around the age of eight weeks, when my siblings and I were still mere balls of black fuzz small enough to sit in the palm of your hand, I was aware of people visiting the house more often than usual. One afternoon I woke from a nap to find that instead of four siblings I had just two. A surprising discovery, but not one that caused me any undue concern. My mother calmly explained to us that our brothers had gone on an adventure to a new home, and if I felt anything it was a pang of disappointment that I had been left behind. A few days later when another pair of strangers arrived, I made sure I was wide awake and on my best behavior—friendly and affectionate with just a hint of reticence thrown in for good measure. Unlike my sisters, who flung

---

* For the record, she also taught me that what black cats lack in cuteness, they make up for in intelligence.

themselves around the room and raced up the curtains in an attempt to show off, I played it cool. The strangers fell for my charm, and for the price of a bottle of wine, I was taken away. (In case you're wondering whether my mother received any compensation for the loss of her offspring, she did: a voucher from the cat charity for free neutering.)

I was lifted into a plastic cat box lined with newspaper, then placed on the backseat of a car between two very excited little people. These were a novelty to me, and quite different from the adult members of their species. They seemed to be all face and fingers, pressed up against the mesh door of the cat box. And their volume control was definitely set a few levels higher than their adults'. But their faces were benign, and I sensed that, like me, their primary instinct in life was to make friends and have fun, so I didn't fear them.

When the car stopped, my box was lifted out and placed in the hallway of my new home. I tiptoed into the living room, and for the first time since my adventure began, I felt a pang of fear. Everywhere I looked there were toys that moved, played music, or jerked unexpectedly into life, usually triggering the excited squeals and yelps of the little people. Faced with this unfamiliar sensory overload, I reacted in the way any sane kitten would—I ran under the sofa and hid as far back as I could, to watch the goings-on from a safe vantage point. I hoped that the little people would forget about me, but instead they seemed to take my hiding as an invitation to play and began to shove toys under the sofa at me in an attempt to lure me out. It is not an exaggeration to say that I began to curse the inventor of the telescopic grabber-arm.

I think I spent most of the day in this position, dodging the onslaught of toys. I must have fallen asleep, as the next thing I remember it was dark outside and the little people had gone. I awoke to find myself surrounded by assorted teddy bears, plastic food, and other childish accoutrements. I must have looked like a feline Lady Gaga impersonator. I extracted myself from the ensemble but remained under the sofa to maintain my lookout position.

After a while I heard the unmistakable sound of a cat flap opening in another room, shortly followed by cat food being eaten, then claws on a wooden floor. The next thing I knew a male cat was lying on the carpet directly in front of my hiding place, beginning his grooming ritual. The cat was a black short-hair like me, but with a white blaze on his chest and white paws. I estimated that he was around three years old. He was tall and slender, with long legs and tail, and he had the most extravagant set of white whiskers I'd ever seen. In my vulnerable emotional state, I was overcome by a feeling of warmth toward him. I realized how much I had missed feline company: it seemed like a lifetime ago that I had been sleeping in a heap with my siblings, being groomed by my mother. I rushed out from under the sofa to greet him, with a cheerful chirrup by way of introduction.

The phrase "jumped out of his skin" would probably best sum up the cat's reaction to my unexpected appearance at his side. Possibly the fastest movement known to the feline world is that of a startled cat from "fully reclined on carpet" to "fully alert on dining table, with arched back and fluffed-out tail." This was the trick that my new stepcat (whose name I learned was Pip) managed to pull off, and needless to say, it wasn't the response I'd been hoping for.

The rest of the evening was spent in a tortuous game of cat chess, in which Pip and I took turns to advance on our haunches for a cautionary sniff, often triggering a hiss or spit from one or the other of us. Then we would retreat to our respective lookouts (me, under the sofa; him, behind the footstool) and eyeball each other until one of us felt brave enough to begin the advance again.

I would love to tell you that at the end of this merry dance Pip and I became firm friends, but we didn't. What actually happened was that I eventually fell asleep under the sofa, worn out by the drama and the pseudo-aggressive posturing, and I think Pip must have stalked off in a huff, because I hardly saw him for the next two weeks. I knew he was around, as I sometimes heard the cat flap swishing or food being eaten in the bowl, but for days on end I saw no more of my stepcat than the tip of his tail disappearing through a doorway whenever I walked into a room.

There's only so long a cat can sulk for, however, and eventually a spell of wet weather drove Pip back indoors. At first he made a show of being upset and angry whenever he encountered me—often lashing out with claws bared if I got too close—but it was obvious that he was milking the situation for sympathy, and he got short shrift from our owners. I probably didn't help matters by playing hunt practice with his tail, but I was only a kitten, and he was fundamentally a gentle cat (although don't tell him I said that). More to the point, he was intelligent enough to realize that fighting me was going to be a waste of energy and would probably cost him the goodwill of our owners.

Pip and I slowly established our rules of engagement. He let me know in no uncertain terms that the laundry basket in our owners' bedroom and the radiator sling bed in the dining room were his exclusive domain, so I opted for the little people's beds and the sofa cushions in the living room as my napping areas of choice. In those early days Pip rarely did more than growl in acknowledgment of my presence.

"Morning!" I would chirrup cheerfully as I scampered to the food bowl to join him for breakfast.

"Hrrmph," he would reply, walking away in disgust.

I eventually accepted that Pip simply was not much of a conversationalist, at least, not when he was with me. He did not seem keen to enter into the lively banter that I have always considered to be essential to life. He had been the family's first cat and was never going to welcome a stepsibling into the home, no matter how charming that stepsibling might be. Clearly, we were never going to be soul mates, but the emotional energy required to hate me wore him down eventually, and after a few weeks, we had established a relationship based on tolerance, if not affection. I stopped jumping on him, and he stopped growling at me.

I found the humans much easier to manage, and it soon became evident that cat/human relations were my natural forte. I learned that there were certain taboos that had to be respected (bodily excretions deposited anywhere other than the litter tray, for instance, and attempting to eat from people's plates while they were in the middle of a meal), but in most other respects they were a doddle. I also worked out very early on that it is, in fact, the little people who rule the human home, and that the key to successful cohabitation with humans lies in keeping on side with the children. Their techniques for manipulating their elders could form a master class in psychological warfare, in particular their ability to get what they want through dogged persistence alone. If they wanted to play with me, I would play, for I had discovered that once I had reduced them to helpless giggles they were putty in my paws. In exchange for a quick session of kitten-trapped-under-a-duvet, for instance, they would happily fill my bowl with cat treats. (And, unlike the adults, they took no notice of whether there was already a pouch of food lying untouched in the dish.)

By observing Pip's behavior I also picked up a few attention-seeking techniques. One of his ploys was the "scratching the TV screen while people are watching it" maneuver, which for a while was an effective way of getting himself a top-up of crunchies, but had to be abandoned when our owners bought a water pistol to keep by the sofa. In retaliation for the soakings he received, Pip came up with his "killer move": scratching at the bedroom mirror in the middle of the night. He was smug about this technique, and with good reason. It had a 100 percent success rate at getting someone to feed him, with the added benefit that a half-asleep human stumbling around at four a.m. was invariably more generous with the crunchies than a fully conscious human in the middle of the day.

I challenged myself to devise a method of waking the humans to outdo Pip's. One night I waited until all the humans were in a deep sleep, and then I jumped onto the wardrobe in the children's bedroom and began to knock toys off the top. I correctly deduced that by waking up the little people first, and allowing them to do the necessary shouting and hollering, the grown-ups would respond just as quickly as they did to Pip's scratching but, crucially, without blaming me for the disturbance. Sure enough, one of them stumbled in to settle the children and—coincidentally—tripped over me at the top of the stairs on the way back to bed. I assumed an air of "just passing," when the thought apparently crossed my mind, "I don't suppose you could top up the crunchies, since you're up anyway?" Bingo. A full meal at three a.m. without the people realizing I was the reason they had been woken in the first place. That's black cat intelligence in action: getting someone else to do your dirty work for you.

It was also quite early on in my kittenhood that I developed my talent for comedy. It was a discovery I made purely by accident, when I tried to run across a freshly mopped wooden floor one morning. A lesser kitten might simply have given up upon realizing that the usual grip effect of its paw pads was failing. I, however, decided to keep running, pumping furiously with my hind legs while my front legs splayed out in all directions, claws desperately scrabbling to grab hold of something. Before long I was adding to my slapstick routine with new tricks, including the "reverse backflip in pursuit of dangled piece of string" and the timeless classic "rolling off sofa while asleep." Seeing the hilarity my antics induced in my owners gave me my first inkling that a career as a performer might suit me.

Around the time I became aware of my own nascent ability as an entertainer, I began to notice another cat with precocious talents. This was a cat who appeared on the television, often several times a day, in a cat food commercial. The cat in question was an orange-and-white tom, clearly in his physical prime, who was filmed in various high-energy pursuits—running underneath a waterfall, jumping over a stream, outwitting a (particularly dumb-looking) dog who was trying to block his way, all to the pumping soundtrack of Destiny's Child's "Bootylicious." Having dodged all obstacles the feline hero rushed through a cat flap into a farmhouse kitchen to feast on a bowl of delicious-looking food. He looked straight to camera in the commercial's final shot as the words "Kit-e-Licious: Are you ready for my chunks in jelly?" appeared on the screen.[†]

This was not the only cat food commercial I had seen, but something about it got to me, maybe because it depicted a world I had yet to experience—the world of the great outdoors. Apart from the journey to my new home (during which I had been enclosed in a cat carrier), I had never been outside.

That, however, was about to change.

After about a month of routine in which I would sleep, eat, play, wash, and sleep again, the cat box reappeared in the hallway, alongside an additional identical one. Before I knew it I was scooped into the familiar-smelling receptacle, and Pip was similarly dispatched into his. Now, this is exciting, I thought, although judging from the look on Pip's face he did not share my enthusiasm. In fact, if anything, Pip looked decidedly downcast. In the car I was placed on the backseat between the children, and Pip traveled up front in the passenger seat. And I hope he won't mind me saying that, once in the car, he cried like a girl.

A short while later we were both placed on the floor of a large room. Unable to see anything other than my owner's legs, I assessed my surroundings using my other senses. Smells: antiseptic, humans, unfamiliar cats, dogs. Sounds: assorted mews and yelps, claws scraping on hard surfaces, Pip's piteous yowling. After a few minutes of waiting we were ushered into a smaller room, where a man placed Pip's box on the top of a table, leav-

---

[†] In case you're wondering: yes, I could already read. I told you black cats are intelligent.

ing me to observe proceedings from my box on the floor. The man (a vet, as you have probably deduced) proceeded to examine Pip, checking his mouth and ears and squeezing his tummy, before finally sticking a needle between his shoulder blades, which I could tell from Pip's body language was not a pleasant experience.

In my cat box awaiting the inevitable, my eyes were drawn to a poster on the wall. It was a photo of an orange-and-white tom smiling at the camera, displaying two rows of gleaming white teeth.

"For a bite that's bright, use Feli-Fang toothpaste!" read the text at the bottom. I'm sure I know that cat, I thought. Then it dawned on me—it was the cat from the Kit-e-Licious TV commercial.

He certainly gets around, I thought, but before I knew it my box was being hoisted onto the table, and the vet's face was peering at me through the door.

My memories of what followed are what you might call impressionistic: a bright light, what I would term "groping" by the vet, a needle. I understood why Pip had looked so morose on the journey over. But it was all over quickly enough and we were soon inside our boxes, being put back into the car.

Perhaps it was a coincidence, but I found that when we returned home, for the first time in my twelve weeks of life, the back door was left open. After three months of doors being slammed in my face and cat flaps being hastily locked, the outside world was suddenly made available to me. I could take my first tentative steps into the great outdoors.

CHAPTER 2

Beyond the Back Door

A bird does not sing because it has an answer.
It sings because it has a song. And because it
is trying to annoy me.

—Chinese proverb (amended by me)

It was a sunny day in early September when I nervously ventured out for the first time. Remember I was only twelve weeks old and small for my age, and until now the outside world was something I had only ever seen from the safety of a windowsill or through the door of my cat box. Now I was at one with the wilderness (or at least, with a rectangle of lawn surrounded by a herbaceous border), and I don't mind admitting that I was daunted by the scale of it. I sat on the patio. I sniffed. I jumped unexpectedly when a loud noise or sudden movement took me by surprise. I sniffed some more. Pip observed my uncharacteristic timidity with wry amusement.

I was mesmerized by the birds in the trees. Allow me to tell my human readers something about the birdlife in your gardens. Their chirps, tweets, and coos may sound like pleasant musical wallpaper to your ears, but to cats, it's a form of aural torture. The dismal, mindless monotony of it! Approximately 80 percent of all bird dialogue consists of:

"I'm here! Where are you?"

"I'm here, see! I'm here!"

"Oh, there you are! I can see you. Can you see me?"

"Yes, I can see you. I've moved. Now I'm over here!"

The utter inanity of it is enough to send a cat into a murderous rage. You wonder why cats kill birds and don't bother to eat them? We're not playing; we're not offering you gifts; we're not suffering from the delusion that we can teach you to hunt; we're just trying to shut the feathery bastards up!

As if the updates about their own location weren't bad enough, I noticed that birds spend the remaining 20 percent of their waking hours reporting on the whereabouts of cats.

"There's a cat! There's a cat!"

"I know! I can see it!"

"It's moved! Watch out!"

"Is it coming my way? Where is it?"

Can you imagine what life would be like if your every movement were noted and discussed by a dozen feathered commentators? Trust me, if humans could understand what the birds are saying, you would want to take the lot of them out with an air rifle.

But I'm not here to talk about the birds. Cats are the plat du jour on my autobiographical menu.

I quickly realized that a handsome gray-and-white tabby called Dennis was our street's alpha cat. He was one of the few unneutered toms in the area and an old-school "unreconstructed male." In other words, he wasn't afraid of getting into a fight. His ears bore the scars of countless territorial battles, and he carried himself with a confident swagger. Alpha cats patrol their domain on a daily basis, spraying at least one point in each garden along the way. Observing this behavior in Dennis, I was struck by the Sisyphean futility of the alphas' ritual. No sooner had a tree been sprayed, but the scent had faded and needed to be resprayed, or another cat had come along and oversprayed it. What was the point, I wondered. What higher purpose was served by this endless spraying? Perhaps, I pondered, from my vantage point on the patio, this was another example of the nature vs. nurture debate. No matter how much you humans "domesticate" us, there are some instincts cats are unable to suppress, and unfortunately for you, it's usually the ones involving bodily excretions. Such questions did not seem to bother Dennis, however, as he aimed his hindquarters at our forsythia and delivered a dose of scent into its branches.

At the opposite end of the personality spectrum from Dennis was Brambles. Brambles lived a few doors down from me and occasionally visited our garden. He was a tabby-point Siamese of small build, with a delicate bone structure. I could see he was a young cat, but there was something of an "old man" quality in the way he carried himself. I would watch him tiptoe down the path with a haunted expression on his face, as if expecting someone to pour a bucket of water over him at any moment. He would embark on a circuit of the lawn, sniffing the shrubs to see who had visited previously, but as often as not the pollen would trigger a fit of sneezing. If he saw me watching him he would smile shyly, before carefully re-treading his steps and making his way back to his own garden.

One day I caught him unawares by the flower beds.

"Hi, I'm Nancy. I'm Pip's stepcat."

He leapt back, startled, then said, "My name's Brambles."

He paused for a moment, looking me up and down.

"You look young. How old are you?"

"About fourteen weeks, I think."

A look of concern flashed across his face.

"I hope you've had your vaccinations. You wouldn't want to catch anything nasty out here."

"Don't worry, I'm fully jabbed up," I replied, to his evident relief. He lifted one of his front paws to inspect his paw pads.

"Urgh, look at that mud. I knew I shouldn't have come out today," he said, more to himself than to me.

"I can't see any mud," I commented—his paw looked pristine.

"Germs!" he exclaimed, making me jump. "Just because you can't see them, doesn't mean they're not there!"

"Oh, okay. If you say so."

Brambles suddenly gasped and clutched his stomach with his paw.

"Gotta go!" he said urgently. "I think my IBS is about to flare up. I *knew* I shouldn't have come out today!"

And with that he scurried through the trellis, not wanting to entrust his delicate constitution to the unsanitary conditions of anyone else's territory.

Hmm, I reflected. I guess I've just met the neighborhood eccentric. Still, at least Brambles actually spoke to me, which was more than could be said for Pip. I knew it would take time to get to know my new feline neighbors, but gradually the pieces of the jigsaw began to fall into place. Who lived where. Who was related to whom. Who once had a thing with so-and-so (usually Dennis—that cat gets around). My human readers probably have no idea of the feline soap opera that goes on in their back gardens. You obsess over your own relationship dramas but remain completely oblivious to what's going on under your noses among your cats. Take my word for it, it's like a human soap opera, just with fur. The feline population of a neighborhood is in a permanent state of flux. Cats move away. Cats acquire step-cats. Cats have kittens. On the positive side, all cats know that it is a rite of passage to be the "new cat on the block." What I didn't realize at the time was that the way you handle your first social interactions on the street will decide your place in the feline pecking order.

Take Bella, my next-door neighbor, for instance. Bella was an eight-year-old calico who was re-homed to our street at age six when her owners emigrated. Bella had a choice. She could either make the most of her chance to reinvent herself in middle age, throwing off the shackles of her old life, or she could dwell on the perceived rejection by her previous owners and mope around feeling sorry for herself. Bella chose the latter. Her conversational icebreaker when first meeting the neighborhood cats was "My owners abandoned me."

Can you *imagine*?

Needless to say, Bella was thereafter referred to as "poor Bella" by most of the cats on the street, which did her self-esteem no favors.

I call cats like Bella "sob-story cats." I'm sure you know the type. They've always got a tale of woe:

"My mother died giving birth to me!"

"My dad is also my brother!"

"I lost my tail in a car accident!"

Pick any street in Britain and you could find tales of feline tragedy and abuse to fill the daytime TV schedules for a year. I don't mean to sound unsympathetic, but we could all come up with a sob story if we wanted to. Happiness is about how you handle what life throws at you. Deal with it and move on.

What Bella's tale illustrated (although I didn't realize it at the time) was that my future reputation hung in the balance. It was all up for grabs. Was I going to be a leader or a follower? A Simon Cowell or a Piers Morgan? You only get one chance to make a first impression, and if you had seen me sitting on the edge of the lawn watching the ants crawl over my tail, you could have been forgiven for thinking I was not destined for great things. A life of mediocrity seemed mine for the taking. Fortunately for me, fate intervened.

On one of my very first expeditions beyond the boundary of my own lawn, I crossed Bella's garden (she was too timid to impose territorial restrictions on others) and jumped over the far fence, to find myself face-to-face with a puce-cheeked Jack Russell. This was not my first encounter with a dog, as my mother had shared her home with an Alsatian. But, as I have subsequently learned, it's the small dogs you've got to watch. Like playground bullies, they choose smaller victims. I was not familiar with "small dog syndrome" at the time, but I could tell from the way a vein on the Jack Russell's forehead was throbbing that he was not about to offer to take me out for dinner. I instinctively assumed the arched back and fluffy tail stance, but to any dog (even one of abbreviated stature) a kitten, albeit at maximum fluffiness, does not pose much of a threat.

Picture us, reader, squaring up to each other in the middle of the garden. It goes without saying that the birds in the surrounding trees were going ballistic.

"It's a cat!"

"It's a dog!"

"It's a cat *and* a dog! Oh, my god!"

Meanwhile, for me, things seemed to be happening in slow motion. The dog's top lip peeled back into a snarl, the vein on his head still pulsing. I glanced around the unfamiliar garden to assess my options. Should I aim for the tree to my right, the house to my left, or the fence behind me? And why wouldn't those birds shut up? Before I had time to make a decision, the dog lunged at me in a frenzy of bad breath and slobber, and without thinking I spun on my heels and dived into a gap under the fence. Being a kitten (and naturally petite) was definitely to my advantage, as I was able to squeeze through the gap without so much as a whisker out of place. My adversary, on the other hand, succeeded only in wedging his head into the opening, finding himself stuck with his body on one side of the fence and his snarling face on the other: the perfect vantage point from which to view me race across Bella's garden and clear the fence back to my home turf in one bound.

In a state of shock, I rushed into the house and headed straight for the sofa, where I did what any cat would do after such a trauma: I had a wash and a nap.

When I woke up, Pip was sitting on the carpet smiling at me.

"So you've met Bruce, I gather," he said.

"Er, I might have," I replied, amazed that Pip appeared to be initiating a conversation.

"Outwitted him, too, so I hear."

I was unsure of how to answer.

"He's got a bit of a reputation, has Bruce. Claims to eat kittens for breakfast."

"Ah," I said uncertainly.

"You did well."

And with that Pip stalked off, leaving me shocked on two counts. First, that I had finally had a conversation of more than two words with him, and second, that I had somehow outwitted a notorious canine cat-hater.

It was not until I ventured outside the following day that I realized the significance of my actions. More cats than usual passed through our garden that morning. In fact, more cats than I had ever seen. They came alone at first, then returned in pairs, all of them casually glancing in my direction.

I could hear them whispering, "That's the kitten who fought Bruce. And *won!*"

Gossip being what it is, by the end of the day my story had morphed into an epic tale, a gladiatorial encounter in which I had launched myself ninja-style at Bruce's face, and he had run off whimpering with his tail between his legs. Having an innate understanding of the benefit of good PR, I did not rush to correct any inaccuracies. The upshot was that my reputation as a fearless explorer was born, and consequently, my place as the de facto "wunderkind" in the local cat hierarchy was established.

Newly confident of my street cred (and knowing which garden to avoid), I began to familiarize myself with the other homes on my street. Many of the houses had cat flaps of their own or left their back doors open in the warm weather. I was bemused to find one house in which three rats were kept in a cage. Amazed at the notion of the world's least popular rodent being kept as a pet, I introduced myself. Bish, Bash, and Bosh were erudite and intelligent and aware of the irony of their vermin status, given their species' superior intellect. They explained that they had made a conscious decision to embrace their life of imprisonment, believing that true freedom exists solely in the mind. I admired their fortitude, though I couldn't help but feel sorry for them, discussing the relative merits of the existentialist philosophers as they sat in sawdust and nibbled a cardboard tube. Thankfully, Brambles seemed unaware that there were vermin living on the street or he would have had a nervous breakdown at the hygiene implications.

I would often find a bowl of cat food in my neighbors' kitchens—a welcome sight for a hungry, active kitten. Sometimes, after repeated visits, the bowl would inexplicably vanish, but after a quick hunt around I would usually discover it on a worktop or sometimes on top of the washing machine. Occasionally it would turn out to be in a wall-mounted cupboard. I was perplexed by this quirk of human behavior, but I was happy to indulge my neighbors' eccentricities. I began to notice how often I would come across the smiling face of the Kit-e-Licious cat as I rooted around in people's kitchens. He was on food packaging, tea towels, even on the food bowls themselves. Remember I was at an impressionable age, and I convinced myself that, somehow, this cat was following me.

After a few weeks, when I was a familiar visitor to all the houses on my street, I began to yearn for a greater challenge. Be it wanderlust or ambition, I didn't have a name for it but I knew I had a calling for something bigger. The mantle of wunderkind weighed heavily on my narrow shoulders and as time went on I felt it was my duty to spread my wings. I was ready to explore the rest of my hometown.

CHAPTER 3

Team Nancy

No cat is an island.

—(Adapted from) John Donne

As autumn drew on I began to venture farther from home (or Nancy HQ, as I was beginning to think of it). My encounter with Bruce meant that word of my chutzpah had spread, and I decided the time had come to set about widening my social circle.

I soon established that my hometown, which lay about twenty miles north of London, was what people call "well-heeled." In other words, affluent. I came to this conclusion not because of the impressive houses and fancy cars that I came across on my wanderings, nor because of the chichi boutiques on the high street (not to mention the cupcake shop called Yummy Mummies). No, my method for measuring affluence was by the proliferation of pedigree cats.

On my street, for instance, which was at the more modest end of the spectrum, Brambles the Siamese was the only pedigree, the rest of the feline population comprising bog-standard alley cats. On other streets in the town, however, I could hardly move for pedigree cats. My theory was that, for a certain type of owner, a pedigree cat was a status symbol, like a luxury car or a designer watch. The wealthier the person, the less likely he or she was to be satisfied with a run-of-the-mill cat. Why make do with a homegrown moggy* when you can afford a rarefied variety of cat with unusual looks and a poncey name? It's rather like Madonna's and Angelina's approach to adopting children, I suppose. The more exotic the better.

The pedigree cats I encountered around town also tended to suffer, like Brambles, from afflictions of mind and body. In Brambles this took the form of an irritable bowel and obsessive-compulsive tendencies, but I discovered that this was just the tip of the neurosis iceberg where pedigree cats were concerned. Phobias, allergies, eating disorders—you name it, a pampered cat in my town had it. That's what you get if you pay two hundred pounds for a kitten, unfortunately. They are beautiful to look at, undoubtedly, but—be warned—you will end up with a cat with "issues." Particularly susceptible to anxiety disorders, pedigrees will often venture no farther than their own garden (sometimes not even beyond their own back door). They don't want to explore in case their fur gets matted, they never hunt because they have sensitive stomachs, and they can be the most dreadful divas. One Burmese that I met would only pee on fresh laundry. If that's not the definition of high maintenance, I don't know what is.

So there I was, small but perfectly formed and, thanks to Bruce, already something of a celebrity among my peer group. But you can't be leader of the pack without a pack to lead, and the way I saw it there was a vacancy for a cat who could liven up the dull lifestyles of these small-town felines. I knew that I was capable of great things, but I also knew that to reach my full potential I would need support, or, in Hollywood parlance, an entourage. As I made my way home one afternoon the penny dropped that what I needed was "Team Nancy"—a group of loyal followers who would back me in my quest for wider glory.

---

* For the benefit of my non-British readers, "moggy" means non-pedigree.

Spurred on by this epiphany I turned the corner into my street and trotted up the pavement, wondering which of my feline neighbors I should recruit onto the team first.

A sinking feeling struck me as I caught sight of Bella crouched on her front doorstep, looking morose.

"What's up, Bella?" I asked, trying to sound upbeat.

"Door's locked. They've gone out. I don't know when they're coming back. Or if . . ." She trailed off, assuming the worst.

"Oh, Bella, come on. They haven't *emigrated*. They've *gone to work*. Just like they did yesterday and they will tomorrow. Cheer up!"

But Bella did not want to be cheered up. No matter how many times she observed her owners go about their everyday routine, in which they *always* returned home at the end of the day, she could not stop thinking that she was about to be abandoned. I know it sounds harsh, but I wasn't sure whether I really wanted Bella in Team Nancy. I wondered what she could bring to the party, other than a pervading sense of gloom. I was looking for cats who would cheer me on and suggest publicity stunts, not sit around moping all day.

Not to worry, I reasoned, there are plenty more fish in the sea. I could see from the pavement that Brambles was in his bed, which overlooked the street from the windowsill in his front room. I suppose my alarm bells should have rung when I noticed the giant pump-action dispenser of antibacterial gel next to him. I jumped up onto the window ledge and shouted through the glass.

"Hey, Brambles. How come you're inside?"

Brambles looked at me in disbelief and mouthed something that I couldn't understand.

"Slime poo?" I mouthed back, at a loss as to what he was saying, and wondering if his IBS had flared up again. He then began a first-class performance of charades: curling his tail around his paw and squashing his nose into a snout, before miming a violent sneeze. I admired the effort he had put in, but was still none the wiser as to what he was saying. I stared blankly at him before hazarding, "Pig . . . sneeze?" Brambles shook his head, rolled his eyes in despair, then put his face to the glass.

"*Swine flu!*" he shrieked.

"What are you going on about, Brambles?"

"Haven't you heard? It's arrived. Fifteen cases in the town already this week. It's an epidemic."

"But, Brambles, swine flu doesn't affect cats. You don't need to worry."

"How do you know that?" he shouted, his blue eyes ablaze. "It wasn't supposed to affect humans, either, and they got that wrong."

At this Brambles pumped a squirt of antibacterial gel onto his paw and began to rub it around his nose and whiskers.

"You do what you like. I'm not taking any risks. I'll come out again when the epidemic has passed. Or when you're all dead and I'm the only one left."

Brambles paused for a moment and stared into the distance, allowing the full horror of his prediction to sink in. Then he took another squirt of gel onto his paw and resumed his manic smearing.

Realizing Brambles would not respond to rational argument, I jumped down from the window ledge. This was not going according to plan. My first two intended Team Nancy members had to be ruled out on the grounds of questionable mental health. Of my friends on the street, that only left Dennis. Surely he was more in touch with reality than Bella and Brambles, I reasoned.

I knew Dennis would be due to pass through our back garden on his daily spraying rounds, so I waited among the geraniums for him. It was not long before I began to catch wafts of his scent drifting over the fence from next door, shortly followed by his footsteps rustling through the undergrowth. I surprised him by jumping out from behind the shrubbery as he approached.

"Dennis, why do you feel you have to spray this bush *every* day?"

He stared at me with incomprehension.

"Because it's there."

As if hoping a demonstration would help, he then lifted his tail and delivered a dose of pungent scent into the foliage, missing my face by inches.

"But think of all the other things you could be doing with your time, Dennis."

"Like what, hiding behind a bush waiting to jump out on other cats?"

"No, I mean like helping me to put this town on the map. . . ."

I trailed off, as Dennis had given me a withering look and sauntered off.

It would be fair to say that Team Nancy still needed some work. It consisted of, well, me. And possibly Pip, but only by default, because he lived with me. I mentioned my plans for stardom to him that evening and he pulled a face (which I was to become very familiar with over time), which could roughly be translated as "You'll learn." Team Nancy was going to require a more organized recruitment drive if it was to avoid becoming a self-help group for every special-needs cat in the district.

The following morning was sunny and mild, so I embarked on my mission with a determined step. I headed to the end of my street and turned right up the hill, onto a street that I knew to be rich pickings for moggies. Choosing a house at random, I leapt over the side gate into its back garden and could immediately discern the presence of felines. I surveyed the garden, ignoring the birds who had spotted me and started up a chorus of "It's a cat! A different cat!"

I noticed a cat flap in the back door, so I ran across the lawn and slipped into the house.

As the flap swung shut behind me I was taken aback to find myself almost nose to nose with a cat who looked remarkably like me. A tom with short black fur and green eyes, who I guessed was around two years old. He smiled at me.

"Hello. Who are you?"

"I'm Nancy," I replied.

The cat looked me up and down for a couple of moments.

"Is that Nancy as in *the* Nancy? Of Bruce fame?"

I smiled and nodded.

"I'm Murphy. Pleased to meet you."

Reader, I can't tell you how relieved I was to finally meet a *well-adjusted* cat. I had begun to despair that there were any in this town. Here was a cat who not only looked like me but seemed to have a similar outlook on life, too, which is to say he was friendly and all his mental faculties were intact.

I followed him into the kitchen, where we stopped to eat a snack (Kit-e-Licious, I noticed) from a pair of cat dishes on the floor. As I was eating I became aware of a growling sound.

"Is that you?" I asked Murphy.

"No," he replied. "That's Molly."

I turned round to see a female calico stalking across the kitchen, her eyes fixed on me. Judging by the way her undercarriage brushed along the floor, I guessed she was middle-aged.

"That's *my* food," hissed Molly.

"Sorry," I said, backing away from the bowl.

"Molly lives here, too," Murphy said, with a faintly apologetic look. "She's my stepcat."

I introduced myself to Molly, who glared at me before glancing at her bowl, glaring at me again, and then exiting through the cat flap.

"Don't worry about Molly," Murphy said. "She's always like that when she first meets someone. Took her at least a year to get used to having me around."

I looked at him dubiously.

"Seriously. When our owners bought a new sofa she couldn't walk past it without growling for six months. Doesn't like change."

He shrugged, clearly as bewildered as I was by this concept.

The jury may have been out with regards to Molly, but I knew immediately that Murphy would become an integral member of Team Nancy. He asked about where I was from, what had happened with Bruce, and what I thought of the cats in the neighborhood. He laughed when I described Brambles's performance with the antibac gel.

"That sounds like classic Brambles." Murphy chuckled. "Whatever you do, don't get him started on his lactose intolerance. He'll never shut up!"

Like me, Murphy knew how to have fun. One of his favorite pastimes was lying motionless near the bird table in his garden, waiting for the birds to come and feed, then springing out and scaring the life out of them. I may already have known that I was destined for great things, but that's not to say I couldn't also enjoy old-fashioned feline pursuits, especially ones that involved tormenting birds. We spent that morning happily engaged in this activity, amused and amazed in equal measure that the birds fell for the same trick over and over. We could hear them in the trees:

"Is there a cat?"

"I can't see one."

"We've made this mistake before. Where are you, anyway?"

"I'm over here."

And so it went on, until one of them would flutter down to the bird table, whereupon Murphy and I would leap out from the shadows and send it flapping skywards, shrieking, "I *told you* there was a cat!"

When we had tired of the birds, we jumped over the gate into Murphy's front garden. As we were sharpening our claws on a tree, I noticed a parked car on the street with its rear door left open. The driver had gone back into a neighboring house to retrieve something, leaving a toddler sitting in a booster seat in the back.

"Kitty! Kitty!" the toddler shouted in our direction.

"I think she's talking to us," I said to Murphy. "I've never ridden in a car without being in a cat box. Have you?"

Murphy gave me a smile as if to say "I dare you" and without a moment's hesitation I dashed down the driveway and hopped into the backseat, to the delighted giggles of the little girl. The car was full of the usual detritus generated by toddlers (soft toys, food wrappers, pieces of infantile artwork), so I was easily able to conceal myself from the adult when she returned. She slammed the door shut and drove off, unaware of her feline stowaway.

It was only a short ride, but I have to admit I got a certain illicit thrill from being unrestrained inside a moving car, compounded by the excitement of the toddler, who shouted, "Kitty! Kitty!" at me for the entire journey. When the car stopped I took a deep breath before jumping into the driver's lap. She let out something resembling a scream, but thanks to my fan in the back, who roared with laughter, she quickly saw the funny side and started to stroke me.

"Where on earth did you come from?" she asked as we all disembarked in her driveway.

I trotted up to her front door and mewed, "Well, what are you waiting for?"

She gave me a quizzical look, then with exemplary compliance unlocked the door and let me in.

From this point on it was business as usual for me. I had been in enough houses to perfect my routine: a quick scan of the living room before heading to the kitchen in search of food.

"Poor kitty, are you lost?" the lady asked, rummaging in the fridge and then placing some cold chicken scraps on the floor for me. As I devoured them I felt her hand slide the name tag on my collar around my neck, and she looked at me dubiously. I knew from experience that, once the name tag had been studied, a phone call back to NHQ was imminent.

As anticipated, my owner soon appeared at the front door and, after much thanking and apologizing, scooped me into the cat box and set off for home. I tried to look out of the car window, to see if Murphy was still outside his house waiting for me, but all I could see from my box was the car's glove compartment. In what seemed like no time at all we were back home and I was tipped out into the hallway, where I meowed for food, claiming to be half starved after my "adventure."

As I settled down on the sofa for a postprandial nap, I reflected on the day's developments. To my mind, events had demonstrated two things. First, that thanks to Murphy, my plan for Team Nancy might be back on track. And second, that my owners were evidently able to retrieve me from any household, regardless of distance. With those happy thoughts in mind, I fell asleep.

CHAPTER 4

Taxi for Nancy

*Every cat is surrounded by a neighborhood
of voluntary spies.*

—(Adapted from) Jane Austen

By October, Team Nancy had started to take shape. Murphy had assumed the role of Robin to my Batman, being an enthusiastic sidekick on adventures around our streets. Pip, unsurprisingly, found the idea risible and made no effort to conceal this from me. I teased him, saying I had ordered a framed Team Nancy membership certificate for him to keep by his bed. For a brief moment he thought I was serious, and was about to tell me what I could do with my certificate, when he noticed that I was stifling laughter and stormed off in a huff. There was nothing that wound my stepcat up more than being teased, I realized. But he was still a member of my team, whether he liked it or not.

Brambles had doggedly maintained his swine flu quarantine, in spite of irrefutable evidence that the town had survived the epidemic with both its human and feline populations intact, so all communication with him had to be conducted through the locked cat flap in his kitchen door.

"I won't have to *do* anything, will I?" was his muffled response, when I had explained my proposition. "Like, go with you anywhere?"

"Of course not. Not if you don't want to," I answered. "I'll be the one doing all the hard work. You're just there for moral support."

I sat on his doorstep, listening to him pace the kitchen floor as he deliberated.

"Well, I suppose, if that's the case, then you can count me in," he said eventually. "But only if Bella joins too." He added hurriedly.

"Great! Thanks, Brambles!" I replied. "I'll go and tell Bella the good news."

Definite class B membership for those two, I decided as I made my way to Murphy's house. But at least they made up the numbers.

Molly still had a face on her like thunder whenever I was around, but, like most of the other cats in the neighborhood, she had become accustomed to me invading her territory. She seemed to have resigned herself to my existence, as long as I steered clear of her food. I therefore declared her, like all the other cats whose houses I visited, to be an honorary member.

It would be fair to say that I was gradually building up my brand awareness among the humans, too, what with my habit of pursuing people on foot or in their cars. I started each day with a visit to the corner shop, where I would scrounge for ham at the food counter before accompanying the shop girl on her newspaper delivery round. All in all, life was ticking along nicely. I didn't yet have a fully formed career plan as such, but I knew there were cats and people out there who needed a bit of Nancy magic in their lives. As the saying goes, "There's no such thing as strangers, just friends you haven't met yet." And I threw myself wholeheartedly into the business of meeting new friends.

NHQ overlooked a park, or "nature reserve," as the humans called it (I told you my town was posh). It wasn't huge, but it had everything a cat could want for a decent session of "in the wild" role play. Areas of long, uncut grass lay at the outer edges, and a stream ran through the middle, next to a children's playground.

For some reason most of my cat friends avoided the park, in spite of its myriad leisure activities. Even Murphy was reluctant to accompany me on my "wildcat" expeditions. I tried to tempt him with accounts of the abundant birdlife, but he showed an infuriating unwillingness to give it a go, citing the feeble excuse that "It's just not for me." It did not escape my notice that Molly was usually lurking nearby when these conversations took place. I asked him once whether Molly had told him not to go with me and he denied it, but I did not believe him, and the swish of the cat flap as Molly surreptitiously slipped out of the house confirmed my suspicions.

As well as being an excellent hunting ground, the park was also a great place for me to hone my talent for feline-human relations. It didn't take me long to realize that the playground was a honeypot of cat-friendly humans. Any woman with a stroller was a dead cert for attention (and possibly a snack), and children invariably adored me. I easily trumped the playground equipment as the park's main attraction in their eyes. If I liked them, I would follow them to their car and let them take me home.

I sometimes caught sight of Brambles in his bed, watching my antics with undisguised horror. He would leap up and down by the window, waving his front paws in an attempt to stop me, but of course I paid no attention.

He really hasn't got the point of Team Nancy at all, I thought, seeing him spread-eagled against the glass one day, as I was driven off in a stranger's car.

NHQ was also well-placed for nighttime socializing. There were three pubs within striking distance, and by sitting on the pavement of an evening I could usually find someone to escort me to one or another of them. The Marquis was at one end of my street, on the corner of Murphy's road. It had an open fire and a garden overlooking the river, and as it was the nearest pub to me, the staff soon came to think of me as a "local." I believe they were quite put out when they found out that I also frequented the Gibraltar Castle.

The "Gib" (to us regulars) was located on the far side of the park and was another excellent establishment for the discerning feline customer. Being a gastro pub, it also served hot food—just the thing for a cat who, even on a diet of three meals a day (excluding wildlife), had the physique of a starving waif and stray.

The third pub in my local triumvirate was the Amble, at the other end of my street. It, too, had an open fire for winter and a garden for the summer. Unlike the Marquis and the Gib, however, the Amble had a dog—an aging black Labrador called Guinness. Guinness was slightly taken aback to find that the pub had a new feline customer. But he was a laid-back animal, and it didn't take him long to go from "Ugh, where did you come from?" (when he first lifted his head from the rug to stare at me) to "Oh, whatever" (as he sighed and lowered his head back to the floor). We negotiated our positions by the fire, and due to his arthritis he was happy to comply with my suggestion that I take the cushioned dining chair and he stick with the rug. Once this was settled Guinness's attitude toward me was "live and let live" (the same as his attitude toward his fleas, I discovered to my cost).

Aside from Guinness's fleas, the downside of patronizing the Amble was that it was also my owners' favorite place to go for a drink. One chilly November evening I glanced up from my chair by the fire to see my owners at the bar, clearly oblivious to my presence. I remained motionless, hoping that they wouldn't notice me, or that if they did, they would have the discretion to pretend that they hadn't. When they eventually spotted me, however, they shrieked my name (causing all the other customers to fall silent and look at me) before marching over and prying me (still pretending to be asleep) from my seat. They then carried me like a baby through the pub, in full view of all the other customers (who were now cheering), and out the front door. Even Guinness had a smile on his lips as he observed my humiliating departure. In this manner I was carried all the way back to NHQ.

I made a point of not looking in the direction of Brambles's house as we passed, but I could sense his eyes on me and vividly picture the appalled look on his face.

Still, though awkward at the time, I was happy to turn such experiences into comic anecdotes with which to regale my team. Pip rolled his eyes in disgust, but Murphy would listen in slack-jawed amazement, and although Molly scowled and claimed not to be interested, I noticed that she would be in the room whenever I recounted an adventure to Murphy. She would pretend to be asleep or washing, but I knew she was listening, and I couldn't help but suspect that, secretly, she envied me.

CHAPTER 5

Milestones

*Only the most acute and active animals are
capable of boredom.*

—Lewis Cass

When I was around six months old, I awoke one morning to find the world had turned white. Having been a summer kitten this was my first experience of what I learned was called "snow." After wolfing down a quick breakfast, I rushed outside. The snow took a little getting used to, coming almost up to my shoulders, but I quickly worked out that the secret of snow mobility was to lift my paws high and trot along like a pony doing dressage. I slowly made my way across the back gardens, looking for members of the team to share my excitement with, but they were nowhere to be seen.

Brambles had just relaxed his self-imposed house arrest when the snow arrived, so we had the pleasure of his company for approximately thirty-six hours before he slunk home to watch what he called the "inevitable carnage" from the safety of his windowsill. Bella too had retreated indoors, arguing that nothing was worth sinking up to her elbows in freezing slush for. Even Murphy was uncharacteristically reluctant to explore.

"Are you joking?" was his response when I told him I was heading to the park, where a noisy crowd had gathered at the brow of the hill.

"It's cold, it's slippery, and it's wet. Sorry, Nancy, no can do," he said as he made himself comfortable on the sofa.

I sighed, disappointed but not surprised. Clearly a cat who liked snow was in the minority. I had little choice but to leave Team Nancy to their radiators and fleecy blankets and head out to join the throng in the park on my own.

For the benefit of any cats reading this who have not tried sledding—you are missing out! What's not to love about being put at the front of a sled, held in place securely by a human, of course, and whizzing down a hill feeling the wind in your whiskers? I felt like Kate Winslet in *Titanic*! The snow had transformed the park into a winter wonderland and everyone there, be they human or animal, was suffused by a warm glow of happiness. And as the only cat I felt like the guest of honor. Dogs were ten-a-penny, bounding around with their tongues hanging out, but it was me that people wanted to share their sled with. I felt like royalty as I worked the crowds, trying to make sure everyone got their fifteen seconds of my undivided attention.

A couple of days into the snowy weather a local news crew arrived, parking their van outside NHQ. I loitered in their vicinity as they unpacked their equipment and soon ascertained that they had come to make the annual "Snow Brings Chaos" news report and to film footage of children sledding while the schools were shut. I did my bit to help liven up their pictures by doing my finest snow leopard impersonation in the back of the shot while the reporter did her piece to the camera.

After about a week the snow finally began to thaw. Patches of muddy grass started to emerge through the blanket of white, and the crowds in the park also melted away. Around this time my cat box reappeared in the hallway, and I was placed inside and put in the back of the car.

"Where are we going today?" I asked my owner as she drove, but she stubbornly refused to give me any clues.

When I was lifted out at the end of the journey, I recognized the sights and smells of the vet's, and my heart sank: another injection.

"This must be Nancy," the receptionist said as my owner placed me on the floor by the desk. "Nancy's here for spaying, is that right?"

I'm here for *what*? I thought, as my owner nodded her assent.

I was handed over to a veterinary nurse, and then I watched in disbelief as my owner turned and walked out of the surgery.

"Er, hello?" I called after her. "I think you've forgotten something!"

"Don't worry, Nancy, they'll be back for you afterward," the nurse said soothingly.

"After what?!" I mewed.

She placed me on the black examination table, and all I remember after that is a bright light, a needle, then darkness and silence.

When I came round my initial feelings were grogginess, soreness around my abdomen, and starving hunger. I realized I was lying in a cage and began to wonder what on earth had happened. After a while a nurse came in, so I let her know how unhappy I was with the situation, especially with the standard of catering (I had not had a bite to eat for twenty-four hours).

"Here you go, Nancy. Some water for you," she said, placing a bowl inside my cage. Reader, I will spare your blushes by not repeating my reply. Let's just say I was sore, I was hungry, I wanted to go home, and a bowl of water was *not* at the top of my list of requirements.

Eventually my owner turned up and I was free to go, although not until something resembling a plastic lamp shade had been fastened around my neck. This was, surely, some sort of practical joke. Not only was I unable to see anything that wasn't directly in front of me, but the device acted as a megaphone around my ears, meaning even the slightest noise was painfully loud. As my owner carried me out through the waiting room we passed a man holding a birdcage containing two yellow canaries. I knew what was coming, but thanks to my plastic ear trumpet the birds' commentary ("It's a cat! Wearing a lamp shade!") was so loud it felt as if they were inside my head. Combined with the hunger pangs I was suffering, it made me feel quite nauseous.

Being unable to look down or sideways also meant that I was unable to see my body, which was infuriating in the extreme, as I could feel an itchy scar on my side that I was dying to wash. I spent the journey home in an understandable sulk, and as soon as I was let out of the box at NHQ, I flung myself around the floor kicking my head-bucket with my back legs until I had managed to pull it forward over my ears. From that point it only took a few more twists and squirms to free myself of it completely. My owner, who had watched my performance with resignation and made only a halfhearted attempt to restrain me, fortunately had the good sense not to try to reattach the instrument of torture. I kicked the offending item away in disgust and headed straight to the food bowl, where I consumed two pouches of food in one go.

The lamp shade debacle was not to be the last of my traumas during this trying time, however. Having slept off the remains of my grogginess, I woke up thinking I would head out to see what the team had been up to in my absence, only to find that the cat flap was locked and the litter tray I had used as a kitten had been placed by the back door.

You've got to be kidding me, I thought as I pawed at the cat flap, mewing pathetically.

Pip poked his head round the kitchen door.

"Wouldn't bother, if I were you. Vet's orders."

"What are you talking abou . . ." But Pip was already walking away.

Am I ever going to get more than one sentence out of that cat? I fumed.

Whatever the "vet's orders" had been, the upshot was that

for the next ten days the cat flap stayed locked, for me at least. I could hear Pip coming and going as he pleased, whereas I was trapped inside, the days and nights melding together in one long continuum of boredom. I was reduced, Brambles-style, to sitting by my front window watching the world go about its business, completely unable to partake. The snow had gone now, and the winter wonderland had been replaced by a steel gray sky and an icy sludge on the streets. My mood wasn't helped by the itchy scar, which, no matter how often I licked it, stubbornly refused to disappear. To add insult to injury, it was surrounded by a large shaved patch, making me look utterly ridiculous.

I couldn't keep the thought from my mind that perhaps I was never going to be allowed outside again, and I succumbed to a feeling of lethargy the likes of which I had never experienced before. I spent many hours on the sofa, often sleeping through the short period of daylight that each day brought, and when I was awake I ate huge amounts of food—a double portion of my own plus anything Pip had left in his bowl. Perhaps some of my readers will recognize the symptoms and understand my actions (although I was unaware of it at the time): it was emotional eating because I was depressed. Overnight, I had lost my independence and my raison d'être. I was no longer an adventurous young cat with a social life and a reputation. I had become the thing I despised the most: a couch potato, a layabout. A house cat.

Team Nancy and my exploits around town seemed like a distant memory, and I couldn't imagine myself ever getting back on track. They say that you have to hit rock bottom before you can start to climb back up, and for me rock bottom probably came the day I discovered daytime television. The children had turned the TV on to one of their usual cartoon channels but then vanished into another room, leaving the remote control next to me on the sofa. Irritated by the manic activity on the screen I figured there was nothing to lose from surfing through the channels.

I flicked past all the wildlife programs—I couldn't bear to

watch anything depicting animals in the wild—and past seemingly endless home makeover series. I ended up stumbling across an episode of *The Jerry Springer Show*. The premise of this show, I quickly ascertained, was to place a dysfunctional family (usually with an explosive secret) on a stage, encourage the audience to hurl abuse at them, and then allow them to go at each other like a bunch of scrapping alley cats. I'm sure you can imagine the effect such edifying viewing had on my outlook on life. If anything is guaranteed to make you lose the will to live, it's watching six hours of back-to-back *Springer*s. But I found them strangely compelling, and they seemed to complement perfectly my despairing state of mind.

One afternoon I was engrossed in a particularly unsavory episode, entitled "Who's the Daddy?" Sprawled out on the sofa, I was waiting for Jerry to open the DNA test result envelope when I caught sight of Brambles on the windowsill, clutching a piece of paper in his mouth. He jerked his head in the direction of the front door and jumped down from the sill, whereupon I heard the rustle of something being pushed underneath the door. I dragged myself off the sofa (not before hitting the pause button on the remote control—reader, I told you I was in a bad way!) and walked into the hallway to investigate.

On the doormat lay a leaflet, slightly crumpled and soggy. I turned it over and read "MRSA: The Facts" on the cover.

"Brambles, I do *not* have MRSA!" I shouted through the front door.

"Better safe than sorry!" he shouted back, running down the path and back to his own, germ-free, house.

Oh, this really couldn't get any worse, I thought as I heaved myself back onto the sofa and pressed play on the remote control.

Watching the histrionics on-screen as the paternity results were announced, it suddenly hit me that, bored and frustrated as I was, things could be worse. At least I didn't belong to any of the families who appeared on *Jerry Springer*. It may sound like small solace, but it marked the turning point for me.

The other consolation during this unhappy period of convalescence was Christmas. I realized that something was up when I saw my owners manhandle an enormous tree into the living room. Even in my uncharacteristically downcast state I was able to appreciate the novelty of having a six-foot fir tree in the middle of the house, especially one that smelled alluringly of fields and fresh air. It was impossible for some of the excitement of the festive season not to rub off on me. I couldn't fail to notice how Christmas had even infiltrated the television, with every commercial break now full of jingling bells, snowflakes, or glittering logos. I became quite an expert on the Christmas advertisements, most of which were fairly unsubtle in their attempts to make humans part with their cash. There was one, however, that made more of an impression on me than the rest.

The scene was a festive-looking living room, lit only by the fairy lights on the Christmas tree. Two female cats slept on the sofa.

A flurry of soot falling from the chimney woke the cats with a start. They looked up, cocking their heads to one side, and stared intently at the fireplace, where two empty stockings hung from the mantelpiece. Suddenly a pair of furry hind legs emerged from the chimney, and with a flourish of his tail, a handsome marmalade-and-white tom dropped onto the hearth. He was wearing a red jacket with white fur trim and a matching pointy hat, and was carrying a small Hessian sack over his shoulder. He reached into the sack and pulled out two packs of cat treats, then placed one pack in each of the stockings before turning to look at the cats on the sofa, giving them a wink and a dazzling smile. Then with one bound he disappeared back up the chimney.

The female cats wistfully watched through the window as a sleigh pulled by reindeer disappeared into the night sky and the tagline "Santa Claws says *Have a Kit-e-Licious Christmas!*" unfurled across the screen

Now, I know what you're probably thinking. Don't tell me

you *believed in Santa*, Nancy! No, of course I didn't. But I did believe that if there was anybody who could persuade me off the sofa and back into being my old self, it was whoever that cat dressed as Santa was. He had a certain attitude about him, a joie de vivre, which reminded me of how I used to be, before everything had gone wrong after my trip to the vet.

The next day the little people woke up before it was light and charged down the stairs at breakneck speed. I followed them, curious to know what the rush was about. I was surprised to find that the tree in the living room was surrounded by wrapped gifts, which the children wasted no time in ripping open. While the little people concerned themselves with their gifts, I happily amused myself with the wrapping paper. It made a most satisfying crinkly sound when pounced on, and there were such huge quantities of it I was able to completely disappear inside, where I could pretend I was a big cat on the savanna again. Albeit a savanna covered in gaudy pictures of snowmen and Santas. Even Pip couldn't resist having a tussle with some of the smaller pieces of paper that lay strewn across the carpet.

Once the children had finished opening their gifts, my owner handed something to me, a net stocking tied with a red bow, containing cat toys and treats. Part of me felt like saying, "Stuff your stocking and just let me go outside!" but I knew that might have appeared ungrateful. I took my stocking over to the sofa and looked through its contents. All the usual suspects were there: a catnip mouse, a plastic ball, and a pouch of food. At the bottom was a bag of chewy treats with a familiar face on the packaging: the Kit-e-Licious cat, wearing his pointy Santa hat. He was smiling. I couldn't resist smiling back.

"Well, hello, Santa Claws," I said in my head. "You have a Kit-e-Licious Christmas, too."

And do you know what, reader? As the words went through my head, I do believe I blushed.

CHAPTER 6

Teenage Kicks

Partying is such sweet sorrow.

—Robert Byrne (adapted from

William Shakespeare)

A few days after Christmas I was sprawled on the sofa about to drift off to sleep when I heard a gentle tapping at the window. I opened my eyes to see an orange-and-white tomcat sitting on the windowsill, smiling at me. I lifted my head to get a better view and realized that it was the Kit-e-Licious cat. He lifted a paw and gestured behind him, where a half dozen reindeer stood with a sleigh in tow. The reindeer were all wearing plastic lamp shades around their necks. I tried to jump up to the window for a better view, but my legs felt numb and unresponsive. Instead, I turned to my left to see Brambles sitting next to me, clutching a syringe.

"Don't worry, Nancy, this won't hurt," he said as he lowered the needle toward me. Then two yellow canaries fluttered down onto the arm of the sofa, cocking their heads to one side as they looked at me.

"Why is she twitching, Mummy?" the smaller canary asked the larger one.

"She's dreaming. Try not to startle her."

"Nancy? How would you like to go outside today?" I opened my eyes to see my owner and one of the little people crouched in front of me, their faces smiling.

I chirruped in disbelief—"Really?"

I followed them into the kitchen where my owner held the cat flap open for me.

"Go on, then, you're free to go."

Reader, she didn't need to tell me twice. I dashed out before she could change her mind and inhaled the chilly air deeply. I headed toward Brambles's house, determined to prove to him once and for all that I did not have MRSA. He and Bella were sitting together on his back doorstep, deep in conversation.

"See, Brambles, no infection!" I said as I jumped down from his fence, but I could see that his eyes were already fixed on my scar and his jaw had dropped.

"What. Is. That?" he asked, horrified.

"It's the scar from my operation. It's a bit itchy, that's all."

"Wait there," Brambles said, dashing back into the house.

"Are you okay, Bella?" I asked, noticing her bottom lip tremble.

"I thought you'd . . . gone," Bella stuttered as a single tear rolled down her cheek.

"Oh, God, Bella, please don't cry. I haven't *gone* anywhere, I was just locked in the house."

"I know," Bella squeaked, wiping the tear away with her paw. "But I'm so glad you're back!"

Just as I was wondering whether I was going to have to hug her, Brambles reappeared, clutching an assortment of sterile dressings and antibacterial wipes. "There you go," he said, dropping them in front of me. "You need these more than I do. For now."

I looked at the two of them: Bella snuffling, smearing snot and tears along her paw, and Brambles's face a picture of anxiety.

"Thanks, guys, I appreciate it," I said, and I meant it. They were, without doubt, a pair of fruitcakes, but they were Team Nancy's fruitcakes.

I picked up Brambles's first-aid offerings and headed out of the garden.

After depositing the dressings and wipes in my kitchen, I felt the need for some rational conversation, so I set off for Murphy's house. Breaking into a brisk trot on the pavement, I suddenly became aware of a strange sensation: my belly swinging from side to side as I moved. A couple of times I stopped and peered between my front legs, wondering if I had inadvertently picked something up off the street. But I hadn't, and I came to the unpleasant conclusion that there was, simply, more belly to swing than there used to be.

Oh, my god, I thought, continuing at a gentle walk, I'm turning into Molly! Definitely need to cut back on the Kit-e-Licious treats from now on, I decided.

At the end of my road I turned the corner in front of the Marquis pub, noticing the blackboard outside, which said, "Celebrate New Year's Eve at the Marquis—book now!"

I could hear a scratching sound coming from Murphy's front garden as I approached, and sure enough Murphy was sharpening his claws on the tree.

"Hello, stranger," I said.

"Nancy!" he exclaimed, running down the driveway to meet me.

"What happened? Where've you been?"

"I went to the vet's for an operation and then got locked in the house for ages while my scar healed. Thanks a lot for visiting me," I added pointedly.

Murphy looked shamefaced, but before he had a chance to make his excuses, I said, "So what've I missed?"

"Nothing. It's been really boring around here without you."

"Well, that's all about to change. What's all this New Year's Eve business?"

"Happens every year," Murphy replied. "The people always have parties to celebrate it. It's tomorrow."

"Parties, you say?" I asked, with a glint in my eye. "I don't know about you, but I *really* need a party. Tomorrow night, eight p.m. If your owners are going out, let's have it here. Invite everyone you know."

And with that I was gone, leaving Murphy looking after me (I imagined) in awe.

Walking back to NHQ I had a renewed vigor. I was free again, I was healthy (if a little overweight), and I had a plan. I was not going to let Team Nancy off the hook this time. The whole world was planning a party and I wanted to be part of it.

I passed Dennis on the street.

"Dennis. Party. Tomorrow night. We'll set off from my place. Spread the word," I said without even breaking my stride.

Bella was crouched on her doorstep, waiting for her owners.

"Party at Murphy's tomorrow night, Bella. Everyone's coming. Including you."

Bella was so shocked she could only nod meekly.

Team Nancy are go, I thought. Just Brambles left . . .

"Are you insane?" Brambles asked, without any awareness of the irony of his question.

"Oh, come on, Brambles, don't let me down. It's just a party. Even Bella's coming. Please come. *For me.* You'll be back home by midnight, I promise."

He continued to look at me doubtfully, weighing up the risks in his mind.

"I can't believe you're making me do this," he said, reluctantly.

"Oh, Brambles, it'll be fun. Please."

"Oh, all right, then. Just this once. And just because it's you."

"Brilliant! Thanks, Brambles. Gotta go, I've got a party to organize."

"But I'll be bringing my antibac gel!" he yelled after me.

The rest of the day was spent on a whistle-stop tour of all the homes with cats in my neighborhood, spreading the word about Nancy's New Year's Extravaganza. By the evening I was exhausted, although I liked to think I had gone some way toward working off the excess weight around my girth. After dinner I called Pip over and whispered, "I'm having a party tomorrow night, Pip. You'll come, won't you?"

"Don't be so ridiculous," he replied.

The following day I kept a low profile at home. Menu, music, seating plan . . . all the usual concerns of the diligent party hostess were running through my mind. When the little people went up to bed I knew it was probably getting near to eight p.m., so I slipped quietly out through the cat flap, under Pip's suspicious gaze.

Sure enough, Dennis, Brambles, and Bella were loitering in the back garden, in varying states of excitement and anxiety. Brambles was dragging a plastic bag containing his first-aid essentials.

"Hi, guys. Follow me. We'll take the back route along the footpath. We've got some more cats to pick up on the way."

We set off, making our way down the grassy verge at the bottom of the garden to the footpath that ran behind, stopping only to untangle Brambles's bag from the various branches it became snagged on.

By the time we reached Murphy's house there must have been at least seven of us, and we could hear several more feline voices murmuring in the shrubbery around the edges of the garden.

"Murphy!" I whispered through his back door. "Are you there?"

The cat flap swung open, and Murphy's face appeared.

"I'm here. Coast's clear. We've got at least four hours."

"Brilliant. Come on, everyone!"

We crept silently into Murphy's kitchen, filing past Molly, who was standing like a nightclub bouncer by the door. She saved her filthiest look for me, the last one in.

"Right, then, let's get this party started!" Murphy shouted, jumping up on top of the fridge and knocking an open box of Kit-e-Licious treats onto the kitchen floor, where it was quickly pounced on by a dozen cats (although, for the record, not by me; I hadn't forgotten my diet). Within half an hour the party was in full swing. One cat was inside a kitchen cupboard; another was scratching the furniture in the living room; Dennis was spraying the coats in the hallway. Brambles had smeared antibacterial gel over a patch of kitchen floor and was rooted to the spot, happy to spend the evening talking to Bella. Molly had appointed herself lookout and was on the kitchen windowsill, supposedly checking for signs of her owners' return, but actually spending most of her time shooting disapproving looks in my direction.

Now *this* is a party, I thought with some satisfaction as I walked past a tabby hacking up a hairball underneath the dining table. Someone had turned Celine Dion on at full volume on the CD player, triggering the more emotional female cats in the room to start yowling along.

Suddenly Molly hissed, "Quiet, everyone! There's movement next door."

The music was switched off and we all stopped to listen to the sounds outside. I hopped up onto the windowsill next to Molly and watched as the next-door neighbors unlocked their car and climbed inside.

"It looks like they're going out. I wonder if that means their house is empty. . . ."

I looked around at my fellow partygoers to see if any of them would take the bait. Murphy smiled and said, "Only one way to find out." That was enough encouragement for me, and I was out of his cat flap and into next door's garden before anyone had time to take Celine Dion off pause.

The neighbor's house had a cat flap, but Murphy assured me that the cat had died a couple of years earlier. I gave the flap a cursory push with my nose to check that it wasn't locked, and it creaked open.

"I'll go first, you wait here," I said and nudged my way through to the conservatory. The house was dark and the only sound was the clicking of my claws on the tiled floor. I padded through the living room, down the hall, and into the kitchen.

I was just getting my bearings in the dark when suddenly the kitchen door slammed shut behind me, the overhead light went on, and there was a lady standing in front of me, her mouth open in shock.

"Who on earth are you?" she asked.

I instinctively deployed my usual tactic in this situation—I mewed piteously—but she was unconvinced.

"I've seen you hanging around with next door's cats, haven't I?"

Her hand went straight for the name tag on my collar.

"Nancy. Hmm. Thought so. You make a bit of a habit of this, don't you?"

I ran to the door and continued mewing, pleading with her to let me go. A phone call home at this point would throw a serious spanner in the works. But my fate had already been sealed, and she was picking up the telephone.

It would not be an exaggeration to say this was a total disaster. Had Murphy realized what had happened? Would the party carry on without me? I was powerless to do anything except sit in this strange kitchen and wait.

About ten minutes later I heard a car pull up outside, and events took on a grim predictability. The doorbell rang and I heard my owner's voice in the hall, apologizing profusely. As the lady handed me over to my owner I made one last attempt to escape, managing to wriggle out of her arms and race down the hallway toward the cat flap, but with two of them in pursuit I didn't stand a chance. I felt my owner's hands around my middle, and although I tried to grip the floor with my front paws, my claws were useless on the tiles.

"Oh, for God's sake, Nancy, can you just give it up?" my owner said with what I knew was genuine irritation.

I allowed her to scoop me up, whereupon I was carried out of the house and down the driveway to the car. My owner had not bothered to bring the cat box on this occasion, so at least I was able to ride unrestrained in the backseat. As we pulled away I saw Molly watching from the window with a self-satisfied expression on her face, and I was aware of a flurry of activity as a succession of panicked cats streaked across the front garden.

"I can't believe you've done this *tonight*," my owner said from the front seat. "You really do pick your moments, don't you?"

I knew it was pointless to argue so I chose to mew in my most heartrending voice. Once back at home I was thrown (rather unceremoniously) into the living room, and I heard the cat flap being locked in the kitchen. I walked to the window to see if there was any sign of the other cats, but my owners pointedly closed the curtains so I couldn't see a thing.

Pip sauntered past me, muttering, "Knew it would end in tears" under his breath.

I sighed and jumped onto the sofa.

"Happy New Year, everyone," I said with a wan smile, before settling down to sleep.

"No dramas today, please, Nancy," my owner said as she unlocked the cat flap the following morning. I hopped through, desperate to find out how the night had ended. As soon as I emerged onto the patio, Bella rushed up to me in tears.

"Oh, Nancy. It's so awful!"

"Steady on, Bella, I know I missed the end of the party. It's not the end of the world."

"No, I mean Brambles."

"What are you talking about?"

"He didn't come home last night! There was such a panic when you got taken away; Molly kept shouting, 'Party's over!' and we all left in a mad rush. I don't know what happened to him. Dennis found his antibacterial gel in Murphy's garden, but he still hasn't appeared. . . ."

She showed me the plastic tube, smeared with mud but still recognizably Brambles's.

"Don't worry, Bella, I'm sure Brambles is fine," I reassured her, but inside, I wasn't so sure.

CHAPTER 7

Homecomings

If any cat has a conscience it's generally a guilty one.

—(Adapted from) Max Frisch

S till no sign?" I asked Bella later that day, although I could tell by her tear-stained cheeks that the answer would be no. We had retraced Brambles's route back from the party, but, aside from his antibacterial gel, there was no trace of him.

"I just don't understand where he could be. This makes no sense," I said.

"He never should have gone to the party in the first place." Bella sniffed. "He didn't want to. It was only because I said I was going. It's all my fault."

"Oh, Bella. It's not your fault."

Although I didn't say it, I knew perfectly well that it was *my* fault. I had persuaded Brambles to go beyond his own territory, not to mention to a *party*, probably the very definition of hell for a cat like Brambles. I had forced him to come because it suited me to have him there. That was the plain fact of the matter. Bella was so wrapped up in her own feelings of guilt that my protestations fell on deaf ears.

Pip, on the other hand, let me know in no uncertain terms that I was responsible for the whole sorry mess.

"Pleased with yourself?" he asked me as he set off on yet another search for clues that night.

I woke early the following morning and headed out onto the street. I could see immediately that there was a commotion coming from Brambles's house. The front door was open and his owners were rushing around inside.

"Quick. We've got to get him to the vet. Now!" one of them said, the panic audible in her voice.

I caught sight of Bella lurking in a flower bed and ran over to her.

"Well? What happened? Is he back?" I asked, catching my breath.

"He's back. I waited outside his back door all night," she said, unwittingly twisting the knife further into my guilty conscience—why hadn't I thought of doing that?

"At about six o'clock this morning I heard a rustling sound. I looked up and saw him limping down the lawn, dragging what was left of his plastic bag. All the contents had fallen out, but he was still clutching it as if his life depended on it. . . ."

Bella stopped to wipe her tears on her paw.

"I asked him what had happened and he just said . . ."

"Said what, Bella?" I asked, trying not to sound impatient.

"He just said . . . Bruce."

At this Bella burst into tears again and I had to conceal a gasp of horror. Of course, I realized now, if Brambles had been in a rush to get home he would have forgotten to avoid Bruce's garden. Instead of taking the route along the footpath he had cut across the gardens, straight into the path of the neighborhood's canine psychopath. A picture of Bruce's puce face popped into my mind, the vein bulging with fury on his forehead.

"Oh, God. Poor Brambles. Is he badly hurt?"

"He's got a bruised belly and a gash down one leg, and most of his front claws have gone. He crawled underneath Bruce's shed and has been hiding there ever since. He must have heard us all searching for him but been too afraid to come out."

"Oh, Bella. Well, look, his owners are taking him to the vet right now. I'm sure once he's been cleaned up he will be okay."

Bella nodded but couldn't stop the tears flowing down her cheeks.

Back at NHQ I dug out the antibacterial wipes and sterile dressings that Brambles had given me after my operation, and which I had carelessly discarded. Clutching them in my mouth I headed back to Brambles's house and deposited them carefully on the mat outside his back door. I knew it was too little, too late, but at least it was something.

I walked back home and went straight to the front window-sill to wait for Brambles's return. I had a wash before settling down to keep watch over the street and reflect on the events of the last few days.

How selfish I had been!

I had wanted a party because it suited me, but I hadn't stopped to consider whether my guests would share my enthusiasm. I had become so self-absorbed since my operation it hadn't crossed my mind that others might not *want* to go to a party.

Team Nancy is all well and good, I thought, but I need to let members join on their own terms.

If only it hadn't taken Brambles getting mauled for me to realize it.

About an hour later I saw Brambles's car turn into the road, and within a couple of minutes his owners were unloading the cat box from the trunk. I rushed out to try to catch a glimpse of the patient. I tiptoed along the pavement, stopping at the end of their path. His owner had placed the cat box on the door-step while she unlocked the front door, and I could see Brambles curled up inside. I don't know if he knew I was there—he didn't look up—but his face wore an expression of total desolation.

His owners were talking about him.

"As long as we can get these antibiotics down him he should be back to normal within a week," one said.

Phew, I thought. It sounded like the prognosis was good, although Brambles's face told a different story.

Later that day I ventured past the front of Brambles's house, hoping that he would be in his bed by the window. I approached slowly, not sure how he would react when he saw me. He was sitting up in bed, which I figured must be a good sign, but as I got closer I noticed that he was totally focused on his first-aid essentials, which he had lined up on the windowsill and was obsessively nudging into a perfectly straight line. As I passed directly in front of the window he glanced at me, but there was only the briefest flicker of recognition before he averted his eyes and returned to his work on the windowsill, sliding one of his bottles a tiny fraction to the left.

I returned home feeling devastated. Not depressed like after my operation—this was worse, because in addition to feeling sorry for myself, I felt guilty about Brambles. Even if his physical injuries healed within a week I knew that the damage to his delicate mental constitution might be irreparable. How would he ever regain the courage to go outside again?

I closed my eyes, wondering what I could do to help him. The way he had avoided my gaze could only mean one thing: my very existence was a reminder of his trauma. The best thing for Brambles would be if I kept out of his way completely.

In fact, I realized, I needed to be away from everyone in Team Nancy, all of whom were upset about Brambles, and most of whom probably blamed me.

I felt a visceral urge to escape from everything that would remind me of that disastrous night.

That evening, as the little people were going to bed, I headed out, but this time I didn't tell anyone in Team Nancy where I was going.

When I woke up the following morning the first thing I was aware of was a splitting headache. I opened my eyes and realized that the sleeping person I was sharing a bed with was not one of my owners. And the bed was not their bed.

Oh, God, what happened last night? I wondered, jumping down to see if I could sniff out any clues to my whereabouts.

I remembered starting the evening at the Amble and telling Guinness about Brambles's encounter with Bruce (his verdict: "That's small dogs for you. Aggressive little bastards, some of them.")

I also remembered sitting on the bar with one of the customers and being fascinated by his drink—a tall glass full of a liquid as silky black as my fur but with a creamy-looking froth on top. The customer said, "Would you like a sip, Nancy?" and then people laughed as I took a few cautious licks from the glass. We repeated the trick several times until I had a sticky coating all over my whiskers and nose, which made the customers laugh even more. Then one of them said, "We're going to the Gib now, Nancy. Want to come with us?" which had struck me as an excellent idea.

At the Gib my new drinking partner and I repeated our "cat drinks from pint" party piece, much to the amusement of the regulars there. After that my memories became very blurred. I knew I had enjoyed myself and felt a surprisingly strong affection for my new friends, all of whom seemed to find me hilarious. It had been so nice to feel loved again and, albeit temporarily, put the drama of the previous days out of my mind.

As I sniffed around the bedroom carpet I could vaguely recall someone at the bar daring me to do something, but what on earth was it?

Then I stopped in my tracks, a sinking feeling in the pit of my stomach.

I put my paw up to feel for my collar, then let out an audible groan. Yes, someone had dared me to take off my collar and run naked through the pub, and, clearly, I had agreed.

At this point my host woke up. He looked momentarily surprised to see me sniffing around his laundry.

"So you're still here, eh? You're quite the binge drinker, aren't you?"

I meowed at him, trying to convey some of my consternation about my lost collar, my splitting headache, and the fact that I couldn't remember where I was or how I had got there.

"There, there, it's all right, cat. You look hungry."

Now that he mentioned it, I was starving. We went downstairs together and while he looked in his fridge for something cat-appropriate I sat on his dining table looking out the window, desperately searching for a familiar landmark.

He placed some ham on a plate in front of me and I wolfed it down, then he tickled me behind the ears.

"Come on, then, time for you to go home."

He opened the front door and I gingerly stepped out, half blinded by the low winter sun, which did my throbbing head no favors. I sat on the doormat looking around blankly, then turned back and meowed at him, trying to convey the fact that I couldn't get home without my owners and he would have to call them, but first we would have to find my name tag, which was on my collar, which was . . . Oh, what was the point? Fortunately he understood enough to get the gist.

"Are you trying to tell me you're lost?" he asked.

"Yes! Yes! Got it in one!" I mewed.

We went back inside and he pulled a thick yellow telephone directory out of a bookcase. "Council . . . council services . . . council animal warden . . . ah, here we go." I didn't know who "council" was, but I hoped it was someone who would recognize me and know where I lived. He picked up the telephone and dialed.

"Oh, hello. A little black cat followed me home last night. She hasn't got a collar. She's tiny—she must be very young" (every cloud, I thought—at least the diet must be working).

"Okay, that'll be great. We'll wait here for you." He gave his address.

"Don't worry, cat. Someone's going to come and get you."

He gave me a few more scraps of ham while we waited and, when that had run out, a saucer of milk—I discovered I had a raging thirst as well as an insatiable hunger.

I was feeling much better by the time we heard a van pull up outside.

The doorbell rang, and a stout woman came in, carrying a rather functional-looking cage.

"Would it kill you to put a piece of fleece down here?" I mewed at her as she dropped me in.

"Thank you for notifying us. We'll take it from here," the woman said to my host before grabbing the box and carrying me out to the van.

"Much appreciated," I meowed at her, and as she loaded me into the van I tried to lighten the tone with a joke. "Home, James!" but she ignored me.

Without so much as making eye contact, she slammed the door shut, got into the driver's seat, and started the engine.

"Could you try and keep the noise down, please?" I mewed beseechingly as she turned up the volume on a CD of soft rock classics.

After a few minutes, though, the hum of the engine and the movement in the van had me nodding off to sleep. As my eyelids began to droop, my last waking thought was Phew, that was fun, but I'm glad to be going home.

CHAPTER 8

Juvie

*It is easy to take liberty for granted when you
have never had it taken from you.*

—Author unknown

I was woken by the scrape of the van's door handle, quickly followed by a piercing bright light as the door opened. My mouth still felt dry but the throbbing in my head had, thankfully, gone.

"Are we there? Thanks for the lift . . . ," I meowed at the stout woman, but stopped upon realizing that we weren't outside NHQ, but in a car park next to a fortresslike building.

As I was carried to the entrance I glimpsed a sign by the door: "Shelter for Feral Cats" it read. What's a feral cat? I wondered.

Once inside I took in my surroundings. The room reminded me of the waiting area at the vet's and smelled similarly of disinfectant. More off-putting than the smell, though, was the noise coming from behind a door next to the reception desk: the yowls and moans of feline protestation. There must have been at least two dozen cats back there, I estimated, and none of them sounded very happy. What on earth was this place?

"Got another one for you, Maud," the woman said to the receptionist as she plonked me unceremoniously on the linoleum floor.

"Young female. No collar. Looks like a stray. And reeks of alcohol."

Do you mind? I thought. I do not look anything like a stray!

I heard Maud sigh, then she tapped at her computer keyboard.

"All right. Thanks, Jo. We've got room for her. Come on, then, you," Maud said as she walked around the reception desk to pick up my cage.

She carried me toward the door to the room beyond, and I braced myself for what was on the other side. Hearing the door close behind us I opened my eyes to see a long room lined with hutches on both sides. The furry faces of the cat inmates peered from every hutch. Suddenly there was an avalanche of jeers and catcalls.

"Ooooh—look what the cat dragged in."

"It's a newbie!"

"And she looks young!"

The cage I was in offered me no protection from the thirty or so pairs of eyes now scrutinizing me from every direction. If you imagine the scene from *The Silence of the Lambs* where Clarice Starling first visits Hannibal Lecter in prison, you'll get the picture. As we passed along the seemingly endless rows of hutches I took a few surreptitious glances at the cats on both sides.

Clearly these were not cats from my hometown. There was not a Siamese or Bengal in sight, just hutch after hutch of cats with varying degrees of facial scarring or with eyes missing. And reader, I will spare your blushes, but let's just say their language was shocking. As they rattled the doors on their hutches Maud shouted, "Shut up, you lot!"

After what seemed like an interminable walk, we reached the last hutch in the room and Maud placed my cage on the ground, unhooked a bunch of keys from her belt, and began to unlock the door.

She swung my cage round as she lifted me up, subjecting me

again to another glimpse of the faces leering at me. Then she opened my cage door and tipped me out onto the concrete floor of my hutch.

Without so much as an introductory tour of the facilities, Maud locked the door behind me and walked off. I could hear the other cats jeering at her as she left.

"Nice skirt you're wearing today, Maud."

"Did you make it yourself?"

"Shame you forgot to look in the mirror."

But Maud remained impervious to their barbed comments and had soon returned to the reception desk, leaving me alone with my fellow inmates.

I won't lie to you, reader, I felt more than a little intimidated by these somewhat "streetwise" felines. I skulked to the back of my hutch, praying that if they couldn't see me, they might forget I was there. To my great surprise, however, once Maud had left the room the atmosphere changed almost instantaneously, and I began to hear chuckles coming from the hutches around me.

"Forgot to look in the mirror . . . good one!"

"Thanks very much. I'd been working on that."

"So, who's for charades?"

I crept forward to the front of my hutch, not quite sure whether I could believe my ears. As I peered through the chicken wire I could see one cat, a particularly terrifying-looking black tom with chunks missing from both ears. He was holding up his paws to the cats in the hutches opposite, all of whom were studying him in rapt concentration.

"Six words," one of them called out.

The black tom nodded, then proceeded to jump up and down and blow on his paws. After a couple of minutes of silence another cat shouted, *"Cat on a Hot Tin Roof!"* and the black tom smiled and took an elaborate bow.

"That's three–nil to our side of the room. Whose turn now?" someone asked.

Whatever next? I thought. Spin the bottle?

Relieved that the cats' attention was no longer directed at me, I turned around to have a proper look at my new living quarters.

"Basic" was the first word that sprang to mind.

The floor throughout was concrete, and the walls were exposed brickwork. At the rear of the hutch was a tiny storage heater next to a cat bed that had seen better days. There was also a litter box, food dish, and water bowl. I sniffed at the stale food rations in the bowl.

Think I'll pass on lunch, I thought. I could not suppress a laugh when I noticed the faded image of the Kit-e-Licious cat on the side of the bowl.

Very funny, I thought. If you're meant to be my guardian angel you're not doing a very good job of it.

I looked up and noticed, for the first time, the cat in the hutch directly opposite mine. He was a haggard-looking black and white tom, with a scar that ran from the middle of his forehead, straight across his eyelid, and down to his cheek. He had said nothing since I arrived, but remained seated on the roof of his litter box, regarding me with suspicion.

I ventured a timid "hi" at him and after a pause he smiled.

"Aren't you playing charades?" I asked.

"I've got bigger fish to fry," he replied enigmatically.

"Do you think I could get Maud to bring me something else to eat? I don't fancy the look of this food."

He laughed. "I wouldn't hold my breath if I were you. She won't be coming back for at least a few hours."

Disappointed as I was, I did not want to waste this opportunity to find out more about where I was, and this cat was the first living thing, human or feline, to engage me in conversation since I had been carried away in the van.

"I'm Nancy. What's your name?" I asked.

"My name?" he said, apparently surprised by the question. "Well, I'm Number 29, if that's what you mean."

"Number 29?" I replied, confused. "But you must have a name as well. What do your owners call you?"

"I don't have owners. None of the cats in here have owners. That's why we're here."

Seeing the confusion on my face he added, "We're feral. Homeless. *Stray.*"

He spoke slowly, as if hoping I would be able to follow what he was saying.

"Well, I'm not feral!" I replied indignantly. "I've just lost my collar, that's all."

Number 29 pulled his lips back into a smile. "Yes, of course you have. We've all tried that one."

As he said it, I heard a few chuckles and titters from the other hutches, whose inhabitants had taken a momentary break from charades to listen to our conversation. "So how long have you been here?" I asked him.

"Coming up to four years now," he replied, and, seeing my jaw drop, he added, "I'm not the longest-serving inmate, though; that's Number 17 down there." He pointed in the direction of an elderly calico who was fast asleep in her bed.

"I was born here!" another voice piped up, a young tabby who looked about my age.

"Born here? But how . . . ? Why . . . ?"

"Now, if you don't mind, I'm going to have a nap."

Number 29 jumped off the litter box and curled up in his bed. The other cats had resumed their game, and I heard one of them say, "Film . . . two words . . . it'd better not be *Born Free*—*again!*"

I sat in my hutch, dumbstruck. Was this another dream? Was the Kit-e-Licious cat about to rappel through the window and rescue me, with or without the aid of reindeer?

A phrase I remembered my mother using suddenly popped into my mind: "When in doubt, wash"; and right now this seemed like my only option.

I began to wash furiously, determined not to dwell on the possible implications of my situation.

It'll all be fine, I told myself. My owners will realize I'm missing. They'll send out a search party or do . . . something.

But in the back of my mind, I wondered whether they would be searching for me. I had gone missing many times before. So many times that my owners had become quite blasé about it, always trusting that the phone would eventually ring with news of my whereabouts. I calculated I had been away from NHQ for about sixteen hours, which was still perfectly within my usual routine. They wouldn't start worrying about me for at least another twelve hours. And when they did, would they know how to find me? I didn't even know if I was still in my hometown.

I sighed, finished my wash, and stepped cautiously into the bed. Its tartan fabric was faded and worn and offered little comfort, but I eventually managed to drift off into a light sleep.

I was woken by a soft but persistent scratching sound. I opened my eyes and looked around. There was no movement in the room now—all the other cats were asleep, worn out by their parlor games.

The sound was coming from Number 29's hutch, although he was nowhere to be seen. His bed was empty, and he was not in his lookout post on top of the litter tray. The sound seemed to be coming from the wall at the back of his hutch.

"Hello?" I whispered. "Number 29, is that you?"

Suddenly his head popped up from behind his bed. His expression was a mixture of startled and annoyed.

"What are you doing back there?" I asked, perplexed. "Is this a dream?"

He paused, clearly deciding how to answer.

"No, you're not dreaming," he replied.

He walked to the front of his hutch and stared at me through the chicken wire.

"Can I count on your . . . discretion?" he whispered.

My ears pricked up.

"Yes, of course!" I whispered back.

"Okay. Check this out," he said, slipping down the back of his bed and starting to push it out of the way.

"What are you doing?" I asked.

"Hang on. Just need to . . . push . . . a bit . . . harder. . . ." And as the bed slid across the concrete I glimpsed something behind it.

On the rear wall of the hutch, the exposed brickwork had been chipped away, and there was now a hole, just large enough for a cat to squeeze through.

"How did you do that?" I asked, somewhere between admiration and horror.

"Claws. And willpower," he replied with a smile.

"It's taken me two years. It's not finished yet. I reckon it should take another six months, then I'll be free!" He said it with a twinkle in his eye.

"Wow." For the first time in my life I was genuinely lost for words.

"What's it like out there, anyway, where you live?" he asked.

"Oh, it's so much fun!" I replied, and his eyes widened. I told him all about my neighborhood, NHQ, and Team Nancy, and he listened in silence, totally absorbed. I enjoyed talking about my life just as much as he enjoyed hearing about it, and I lost track of time for the first time since I had arrived at the shelter. We were eventually interrupted by the jangle of keys on the other side of the door, so I jumped back into my bed, and he hurriedly pushed his back into position.

Maud reappeared, this time carrying an industrial-sized sack of dry cat food. As I had suspected, there was no sign of the Kit-e-Licious cat on the packaging.

"Right, you lot. Dinnertime."

She began working her way down the hutches, sprinkling the dry food into the bowl in each, ignoring the jibes raining down on her from all sides.

"I'll have the smoked salmon today, Maud."

"Mine's the duck à l'orange!"

"Take your time, old lady. Don't rush!"

When she eventually got down to my end of the corridor, I

watched as she opened Number 29's hutch and poured out his allotted rations, oblivious to the act of subterfuge that was taking place under her nose. Number 29 saw me watching and winked.

Then it was my turn. I didn't even bother to meow as Maud opened the door and messily poured out the biscuits, half of which missed the bowl completely and spilled all over the floor. I gave them a sniff, but even fresh from the pack they smelled no more appetizing than the stale ones that had been there since I arrived.

How can anyone end up here for four years? I wondered. What kind of life is that for a cat?

I tried to suppress an image of myself in four years' time, marking off the days of my incarceration on the wall of my hutch, praying for the moment when my owners would turn up, in tears and begging for my forgiveness. Surely that wouldn't— couldn't—happen to me, would it?

I looked disconsolately at my food bowl, ignoring the cheesy grin of the Kit-e-Licious cat on the side.

Still, if I am going to be here for a while, I thought, I shall have to eat something.

I reluctantly picked a few biscuits out of the bowl, crunching them between my back teeth. They were dry, as I'd feared, and with no discernable flavor.

Shortly after we had finished our "dinner" the familiar sound of jangling keys alerted us to another imminent visitor. This time it was a man, carrying a yellow handheld device that reminded me, with a pang of homesickness, of the plastic toys the little people had at NHQ. At his appearance all the other cats suddenly became animated, stretching up at the entrance to their hutches and yelling, "Scan me! Scan me!"

"What's going on?" I shouted to Number 29 over the din.

"He's the scanner man. If he scans you and it beeps, that's your ticket out of here. It's never worked on any of us but once in a while it happens. Looks like he's heading your way."

Sure enough, the man was walking in my direction.

"I'm over here! I'm over here!" I shouted at the top of my voice, climbing up the chicken wire door to attract his attention.

He checked the number on my hutch.

"Right, then, little girl. Let's see if you belong to anyone."

He held me under the belly while running the yellow scanner up my back. The other cats had fallen silent, waiting with baited breath to see if the device beeped. As the scanner passed over my shoulders, a clear, unmistakable "Beep! Beep!" sounded and the room erupted into a frenzy.

All the cats in the room were celebrating for me, shouting "She beeped! She beeped!"

The man checked the back of the scanner and raised his eyebrows in surprise.

"Well, look at that. Let's go and find out where you live."

And with that he left the room. I looked around, bemused.

"What just happened?" I asked Number 29.

"It's called a chip. Don't ask me how it works. All I know is that I don't have one. But it means they'll be able to find your owners."

I almost didn't dare let myself believe it.

I spent the next hour in a state of nervous excitement, straining to hear any sounds coming from the other side of the door. Eventually I heard voices in reception, and then Maud's keys in the lock.

"She turned up this morning," Maud was saying. "Had followed someone home. There was no collar."

Then I heard the sweetest sound imaginable, my owner's voice, apologizing as usual, trying to make excuses for me.

"She did have a collar—she must have lost it. Thank you so much for contacting us." And then she appeared in front of my hutch, smiling with relief.

"There you are, you naughty girl! What have you been up to this time?"

"I'll tell you later—just *get me out of here!*" I shouted back at her as I hung off the hutch door.

I had never been so happy to climb inside my cat box, with its familiar smell and newspaper lining. As my owner carried me away I peeked out at the other cats. They were all yowling and catcalling again, but this time I knew not to be afraid.

As we passed his hutch, Number 29 gave me a conspiratorial wink and whispered, "See you on the other side!" I winked back and lifted my paw to wave, but he had already started pushing his bed to one side, ready to begin the final phase of his own escape.

I was welcomed back to NHQ by a pair of ecstatic little people who excitedly showed me the brand-new collar and name tag they had for me. After the collar had been fitted I was given a fresh pouch of food—the tastiest meal I had ever eaten—and then I was straight out through the cat flap.

Just wait till Murphy hears about this, I thought, already working out in my mind how best to tell the story for comic effect.

I was aware of my owner looking at me intently as I trotted past the kitchen window, but it didn't cross my mind that she might have plans for me of her own.

CHAPTER 9

Local Hero

Some cats obtain fame, others deserve it.

—(Adapted from) Doris Lessing

A few days later I was on the footpath behind the garden when I heard my owner's voice at the back door, calling me.

"Ah, there you are," she said as I trotted down the garden.

I chirruped at her, "Well, what do you want?"

"Your presence is required inside, Nancy. You're going to be famous!" she said with a grin.

I followed her through the kitchen into the front room, where a man was unpacking a large camera from a black bag.

"So where do you want her?" my owner asked.

"By the window would be great," the photographer replied.

I jumped up onto the windowsill, and as the photographer's lens clicked I followed his directions to the letter.

"Look as if you want to escape, Nancy." So I looked longingly at the park.

"Look inquisitive, with an undertone of mischievous," he prompted, so I composed my face into a picture of mischievous inquisitiveness.

"Now look straight into the camera, and do me your best frustrated yet intrigued."

I duly obliged.

"That was fun," I meowed to my owner when the photographer had left.

She seemed happy with my performance and opened a cat food pouch by way of reward.

"Well, what did you make of that, Nancy? You're going to be in the paper!"

In the what? I thought as I tucked into my lunch.

It was lamb chunks in jelly, my favorite.

Afterward I set out to resume my tour of the back gardens, turning right, toward Brambles's house. He had remained under house arrest since "the incident," hardly moving from his bed by the window, so my heart lurched when I caught sight of him sitting on his back doorstep.

I took a deep breath, wondering whether I should turn and run, in the hope that he hadn't noticed me. But I knew that things could not be made right until I had apologized, so I waved my paw and tried to catch his eye.

When he saw me he smiled, and, almost purring with relief, I jumped down from his fence and walked over.

I sat by his side on the doorstep and, being British, we talked about the weather. When we had exhausted this topic and had sat in awkward silence for a few moments, I blurted out, "You know, Brambles, I'm really sorry about what happened after the party. I never should have made you go."

He looked into the distance, apparently studying the foliage on the far side of the garden.

After a pause he said, "That's okay, Nancy. It wasn't your fault. And besides, you've got to experiment once in a while, if only to work out what your limits are."

I nodded, inwardly amazed that his response was so sanguine.

"But, for the record, I won't be upset if you don't invite me to your next party."

He turned to face me and smiled.

"Sounds like a good arrangement to me!" I laughed. "So are you back on Team Nancy?"

"Of course. Founding member," he replied with a chuckle.

Then there was another silence, during which Brambles began furiously scratching one of his shoulder blades, and I was seized by an urgent need to wash my hind leg.

Once we had washed and scratched the awkwardness away, I stood up to go.

"You coming?" I asked.

A frown of anxiety appeared on his brow as he contemplated the patio.

"You go on. I'll be right behind you. One step at a time and all that."

I jumped back up onto the fence and turned to look at him. He was making his way slowly across the patio, trying to avoid all the cracks between the stones—not easy on crazy paving. If one of his paws touched a crack he would wash the paw furiously at a snail-like pace, each paw hovering before making contact with the stone.

As I slipped out of Brambles's garden, I felt as if a huge weight had been lifted from my shoulders.

Only now that we had talked could I finally let my conscience rest. I had been amazed by the dignity and, dare I say it, sanity of Brambles's response. I had underestimated him.

Of course it would take time for him to get back to normal, or at least, as normal as it was possible for Brambles to be. As he had said himself, "one step at a time." But I felt optimistic that he was going to be okay.

A few days later I was woken by the little people jumping up and down in excitement. "It's Nancy! It's Nancy!" they shouted.

"Look, Nancy, you're on the front page!" my owner said, spreading the local newspaper out on the dining table.

I jumped up and, sure enough, there I was, pulling my "inquisitive yet mischievous" face, under the headline "Nancy feline fine after hitching lifts" (as I was to learn, journalists are unable to resist a cat-based pun). The piece took up the whole front page, detailing some of my recent exploits, combined with some despairing quotes from my owner. It ended with an (unnecessary, in my opinion) appeal to the residents of my town to look out for me in their homes and cars.

"Front-page news, Nancy!" my owner said, tickling me under the chin. "I guess it was a slow news week!"

I chose to ignore her sarcasm but made a point of walking in front of her face and wafting my bottom under her nose, until she stood up to go.

Once I had got over the shock of seeing myself in print (it's true what they say about the camera adding five pounds) I decided that I came across rather well in the article. In addition to my owner, the landlady from the Amble had also been interviewed, referring to me as the pub's "popular furry punter." Adventurous and charming is how I would sum up my press persona, although a journalist would probably prefer "bursting with *cat*itude." Either way, I sounded like a cat who was going places. In every sense.

"Murphy, you'll never guess what . . . ," I said as I ran through his kitchen to tell him my news. There was no need, however. Murphy was sitting on the doormat by the front door, staring at the newspaper, which had just fallen through his letterbox.

He was spellbound by it and said breathlessly, "It's you! On the front! Of the paper!"

"Indeed it is." I laughed.

"That's *awesome!*" he exclaimed.

Meanwhile Molly slept in her radiator hammock, oblivious.

In the days following my front-page scoop, my owners took endless calls from journalists—some of them from the national press—and more photographers arrived to take my picture.

I became such a pro at being photographed that I would pre-empt the photographers' instructions, able to turn on "inquisitive yet mischievous" at the flick of a switch.

One of the national tabloids ran the story with a photo of me in the car, under the headline "Tabby gets taggy," in which they claimed I was to be fitted with an electronic tag in the manner of a delinquent teen.

Now forgive me for splitting hairs here, but—do I look like a tabby?

Further evidence, if any were needed, that journalists hate to let the facts get in the way of a good pun. (And, for the record, it would take more than a tag to make me adhere to any curfew.)

Inaccuracies aside, I took this newfound notoriety in my stride. I did occasionally suspect that my owners might have regretted their decision to get the press involved. I heard one of them muttering that he was feeling like "bloody Amy Winehouse's dad" after he had spoken to yet another news agency asking for quotes about my tearaway behavior.

The effects of my new media profile reached beyond NHQ, and Team Nancy could not help but get caught up in some of the surrounding hysteria.

Brambles was, predictably, concerned about the increase in visitor numbers to the street once tourists started coming to do the "Nancy Tour," fretting about the impact on air pollution.

Pip seemed to find the whole thing faintly amusing, letting slip the odd barbed comment.

"Well, this is your fifteen minutes of fame, Nancy. Enjoy it while it lasts."

"It's more than you've ever had," I hissed back.

Molly, of course, remained impervious. She refused to read any of the cuttings (which Murphy had helpfully started to compile in an album), or, at least, she claimed not to have read them.

The biggest change was in Dennis's behavior. Out of the blue he started hanging around the garden at NHQ and yowling outside the house if I was in at night.

I admit I was flattered by the attention, and so we went on a few romantic walks around the neighborhood (albeit interrupted every five minutes to allow him to spray).

One evening when I returned from such a walk, Pip cornered me in the kitchen.

"Where've you been, Nancy?"

"Out with Dennis. Why?"

He looked concerned.

"You do know he's got something of a . . . reputation, don't you?"

I looked at Pip, waiting for his face to break into a smile.

"Pip! I do believe you're worried about me!" I said, starting to laugh. "Is this like a big-brotherly chat? Are you going to tell me to be careful and take precautions?"

I was laughing out loud now, enjoying Pip's evident discomfort.

"No, well, yes, well . . . Look, all I'm saying is, you're not the first cat Dennis has done this with. So don't come crying to me when he's got bored of you and moved on to the next one."

And with that he stormed out, no doubt wishing he'd never broached the subject in the first place.

It was probably mean of me to make fun of Pip's concern for my emotional well-being, but I did so because I already knew there would never be a future for Dennis and me.

It was partly because, as Pip had pointed out, monogamy was not one of Dennis's strengths, but also because I had already realized that, macho bluster aside, Dennis was actually quite boring.

First of all there was his habit of glazing over if I talked about anything other than him, and then there were the endless stories of fights he had had with other toms (and always won, of course) or adventures that had involved a combination of superfeline strength and dexterity.

After a while I found it difficult to stifle a yawn when he launched into an anecdote with, "Have I told you about the time when . . ."

In addition to his narcissistic tendencies was the rather more pressing issue of him spraying the downstairs of our house at night. This did not bother me particularly, but my owners were not amused, and I could tell Pip was furious.

Another nugget of advice that my mother had given me came to mind: "Don't shit on your own doorstep" and when, for the fifth morning in a row, the little people's first words upon coming downstairs were "Ugh! What's that smell?" I came to the conclusion that it was time to bring my romantic entanglement with Dennis to an end.

"What do you mean, *you* don't want to see *me* anymore?" he said, looking genuinely dumbfounded.

"I just think we're better off as friends," I explained, aware that it sounded flimsy.

"Hmm. Whatever. Let's call it a mutual decision."

"Okay, Dennis," I said, unable to resist adding, "you seem heartbroken."

He looked at me, not sure how to respond, then turned his bottom to face me and sprayed the tree behind, narrowly missing my face. Then he walked off without a backward glance.

"*Whatever* to you, too," I muttered, although he was already through the trellis and into the next garden.

A more fragile cat might have been hurt by his apparent indifference, but I didn't take it personally. I knew that Dennis had only shown an interest in me because he thought I made him look good—a celebrity girlfriend being the ultimate trophy for an alpha male.

My heart remained intact, and I was happy to chalk this one up to experience.

The phone calls from journalists eventually fizzled out, but thanks to the newspaper coverage, my profile around town was now officially that of "famous cat." The pubs were known to be my hangouts, so it was impossible for me to pop into any of them for a swift saucer of milk or restorative nap without being greeted with a cheer from the staff or customers.

So this is celebrity, I thought.

There were occasional inconveniences, but overall it was a pretty enjoyable experience. On balance, it was something I thought I could get used to.

❧

One cold rainy afternoon in early February I was on the sofa, just coming round from a postlunch nap. As I twisted onto my side to stretch, my eyes came to rest on the television.

On screen was a commercial in which a young, attractive woman was getting ready for a romantic date.

She set the table for a meal, putting out gleaming silver dishes for two, lighting a candle, then applying lipstick in the mirror. The woman dimmed the lights and looked at the clock.

At eight p.m. exactly, the cat flap swung open and in rushed the Kit-e-Licious cat, his eyes gleaming, wearing his most dazzling smile. The woman stroked his ears, delighted. He jumped up onto the dining chair and looked expectantly at his place setting.

The woman took his dish into the kitchen and reappeared a few moments later, setting his meal down in front of him with an indulgent smile.

He glanced at the food, sniffed it, then looked up at her, his face a mixture of disappointment and disgust.

She looked horrified, but before she could say anything he had turned tail and run out through the cat flap, leaving it swinging in the breeze behind him.

Over a close-up of the woman's distraught face, the tagline rolled across the screen: "Serve him Kit-e-Licious this Valentine's Day. Because he's worth it."

Damn it, I thought. Who *is* that cat? He gets all the best jobs.

I could have been in that advert! *I'm* worth it, too!

I could have pulled off "disappointed and disgusted" just as easily as I can do "inquisitive yet mischievous."

And *another* thing—my internal rant was now in full flow—
I've been in the houses of a lot of women who go crazy for their
cats, but I've never come across one as attractive as her! Where
were the hand-knitted cardigans, the threadbare furniture, the
bird's-nest hair?

As I sat ruminating on the commercial's shortcomings, it
dawned on me: why *couldn't* I be in a commercial like the Kit-e-
Licious cat?

There must be a way of getting from where I was, fuming on
my sofa, to being *on-screen*.

Even the Kit-e-Licious cat must have started somewhere.
How had he gone from being a mere pet to being spokescat for
the country's number one cat food brand?

And would I be able to do the same?

I didn't yet have the answers. But thanks to the local papers,
I had made a start on my career as a celebrity. Now I was going
to have to take it up a notch or two.

CHAPTER 10

Mog Blogs

*A cat must have a room and a laptop of her
own if she is to write.*

—(Adapted from) Virginia Woolf

Put yourself in my shoes. (I know I don't have shoes. It's a
metaphor.) I was a cat. A talented one, I grant you, but a cat
nonetheless.

Thanks to my appearance in the newspapers I was what you
could call a "local celebrity."

But as a cat, what could I do to take my career to the next
level? I could hardly phone up MTV and pitch a no-holds-
barred reality show about my life.

How the Kit-e-Licious cat had launched his career was a
mystery that consumed my every waking moment.

I tried to share my frustration with Murphy, but he couldn't
understand why I wanted a career in the first place.

As far as he was concerned, what more could a cat want from
life than a nice home, good friends, and food on demand?

"But, Nancy, what else do you need?" he asked.

"It's not about what I *need*, Murphy, it's about what I *want*.
Aren't you curious about what's out there? There is a world beyond our town, you know."

I could tell he was hurt, that he had taken my dissatisfaction with life as a criticism of him.

There was an awkward silence until I took pity on him and said, "Shall we go and scare the birds?"

He smiled and jumped up. "Great idea!"

So we spent the rest of the morning lurking near the bird feeder, taking turns to leap out at the few unsuspecting avians who had not migrated for the winter.

I did my best to hide it from Murphy, but my heart wasn't in it. What had been one of my favorite leisure pursuits had lost its appeal.

It sounds silly to put it all down to the Kit-e-Licious commercials, but I felt as if I had glimpsed another life and would not be happy until I had taken my best shot at achieving it.

I was starting to feel like I had more in common with Bish, Bash, and Bosh, the caged pet rats on my street, than with my cat friends.

Like them, I had become aware of the limitations of my condition, my imprisonment by the circumstance of having been born an animal.

But unlike them, I could not embrace my fate. It was not enough for me to sit around intellectualizing about my dilemma. I wanted to do something about it.

I had plenty of ideas about *what* I wanted to do, but when it came to *how* I would start, I drew a blank.

A voice in my head whispered, "You're just a cat. Forget it."

It was my owners who gave me my first breakthrough.

Unbeknownst to me, since my appearance in the papers they had also been thinking about my future.

I had kept up my usual antics around town, visiting, among others, the air cadets, the school, and the old people's home, and it would seem that my owners had started to tire of the phone calls and pajama-clad pickups at all hours of the night.

One afternoon my owner called me into the upstairs study. She sat down at the desk and turned on the laptop computer.

"Look, Nancy," she said.

I sat on the desk, watching her fingers as they tapped the keys. Then I looked up at the screen. There was a photo of me, my name, and some personal information. At the side of the screen was a list of "friends," including my owners and some people whose faces I recognized from the neighborhood.

I looked at her, bemused.

"I've put you on Facebook, Nancy," she said, as if that were sufficient explanation. "You've got eight friends already. This way, you can keep in touch with people and they won't have to ask me what you're up to all the time. And, hopefully, it might even keep you off the streets for a bit."

A cynic might say that she had her own interests in mind rather than mine, but I was too intrigued to be cynical.

She gave me a brief tour of the Facebook site, and then left me to it.

I must admit it took a while to get used to the keyboard and mouse, which, in spite of its cat-friendly name, was not very cat-friendly to use.

But once I had mastered the mechanics, I was away.

My first status update read, "Nancy iS HUngrY" (damn that caps lock button—I didn't notice my mistake until I'd already pressed "share").

Then I sent a message to my owner: "MORE FOOD" (caps lock had its uses, I realized).

I sat back and waited. What now?

Suddenly a tiny thumbs-up symbol appeared beneath my status. One of my friends had "liked" what I had written!

Then a message appeared on the screen from my owner:

"Later! Or, feed yourself."

I smiled and typed in a new status update:

"Facebook: where have you been all my life?"

Within minutes I had four thumbs-up symbols.

I must have spent the next two weeks practically glued to the laptop. Acquiring friends proved surprisingly easy, and it was much quicker online than the old-school approach of pounding the streets.

Just a few clicks and new friends would appear from the ether: "You have received 6 friend requests" or "8 people confirmed you as a friend."

Unlike Team Nancy, these weren't just friends in my hometown. They lived all over the country, from Bournemouth to Chesterfield, and they would suggest me to their friends, so that soon I was spreading like a virus across the nation's computers.

Pip sauntered past the study door one afternoon as I tapped away on the keyboard.

"Hey, Pip," I called out, "check out how many friends I've got!"

He rolled his eyes and headed into the bedroom.

"You're just jealous," I called after him.

"It's not real!" came his muffled response from inside the laundry basket.

The best thing about Facebook was that, for the first time in my life, I was able to communicate with humans as an equal. Not having to rely on a human's ability to translate my mews and chirrups into English was liberating.

I had finally found my voice, and my human friends loved it!

In fact, they couldn't get enough of me. It was as if they had never realized that a cat could be witty, urbane, and erudite.

My friends tally was growing—in a matter of weeks I had gone from having eight friends to having seventy. And I had started to acquire friends abroad. First I picked up one in South Africa, then a couple in Australia, then a few in the United States, Indonesia, and Thailand.

My status updates had started as straightforward accounts of where I had been and what I was doing, but I soon began to tire of this approach. (How many times can you type "eating Kit-e-Licious for lunch" and expect people to be interested?) So I started trying out different material: jokes, recipes, even romantic advice, analyzing which posts got the biggest response from friends.

One morning when I had worked my way through a stack of friend requests and messages, I came across a link to a page called Online Felines.

"What the . . . ?" I murmured. "Are there other cats out there on Facebook?"

Scrolling down the page, I could not believe my eyes.

There were page after page of cats, each with its own Facebook profile just like me. I clicked on a few to see what they were like and my jaw dropped. These cats had friends numbering in the thousands, not dozens.

Where were all these cats? I wondered. Did any of them live near me?

I scrutinized their personal information and a pattern started to emerge. These were all *American* cats. There was I, thinking that I had broken the mold, being the first and only cat on Facebook, but no—quite the reverse was true.

In America, it seemed, it was harder to find a cat who was *not* on Facebook than one who was.

I sent friend requests to as many as I could, only stopping when a message popped up warning me not to send friend requests to people I didn't know.

"How come there are so many of you on here?" I asked one of my American friends.

"I'm an only cat. It's the only way I can meet other cats," she messaged back.

"Don't you have friends in your neighborhood?"

"I can see other cats from my window but I'm not allowed out so I don't know them."

"Have you been to the vet?" I typed, assuming that she was recuperating from an operation.

"No, I'm a house cat. I never go out."

"What do you mean you *never* go out? You're a cat. What do you do all day?"

"I have a perch. And a catnip mouse."

"You have a *what*?! Did you say a *perch*? Like a *bird*?"

"Kind of. My owner says it's safer this way."

I had thought I had it bad, living in a small town on the outskirts of nowhere, but this was something else!

I inquired of my other Stateside friends whether they were allowed outside and almost all of them replied in the negative.

"I live in an apartment on the thirtieth floor."

"My sister was killed by a coyote."

"My owner paid a fortune for me and is worried I'll be stolen."

"Well, no wonder you're all on Facebook," I typed back. "You must be bored senseless!"

"Yes, but at least we're safe," one commented.

A fair point, I suppose, but it did not strike me as much of a consolation.

"You should check out my blog," said one. "It's called the Secret Diary of a House Cat."

So, just when I thought I'd made enough shocking discoveries about cats on the Internet, here was something else to stop me in my tracks.

Some cats had blogs!

I spent a couple of days delving into the cat blogging community and quickly realized that, like their human equivalents, cat bloggers were a mixed bunch in terms of ability. For the most part, their entries were humdrum—the banalities of day-to-day feline life, illustrated by a photo or two.

"This is me asleep on the couch."

"Here I am with a paper bag on my head. LOL."

I also discovered a propensity among the bloggers for poor grammar and deliberate misspelling of words in a quasi-phonetic style:

"I iz starvin wotz fur brekfust."

I daresay whichever cat first came up with this idea thought it was cute, the conceit being that cats are unable to master the nuances of the English language, or the intricacies of the QWERTY keyboard, or both.

But when you are reading the tenth blog of the day and they have all been written in such a way that you have to repeat each sentence three times, out loud, in order to make sense of it, the novelty begins to wear off.

Enuff, alreddy.

Clearly I was going to have to start my own blog and show these other felines that poor spelling does not a blogger make. We all know cats can write just as well as anyone else, so let's stop perpetuating the myth that we're illiterate.

My mind was made up. I would write a Mog Blog with a difference. One that would appeal to humans just as much as it would to cats. And that would be grammatically correct.

When I had finalized the layout, typed my first entry (a drily witty account of a recent visit to the local Cub Scouts), and uploaded a photo, it occurred to me that I should encourage Team Nancy to sign up as my followers.

When I headed outside, the temperature took me by surprise. It was now mid-March, and the wintry weather had given away to the first mild air of the spring. I had become so absorbed in my online life recently that I had become oblivious to the world beyond my laptop.

I sniffed the air, thinking how pleasant it was not to feel the sting of a cold wind on my nose, and began to make my way toward Murphy's house.

Of all my friends, I reasoned, he would be the most excited to hear about my blog.

As I trotted along the footpath I passed Dennis heading in the opposite direction.

"All right, Dennis?" I called.

"Hmm," he grunted.

Dennis still hadn't forgiven me for dumping him, apparently.

Never mind, it'll make great material for a blog, I thought.

"Murphy. Are you in there?"

I peered through the cat flap. I was surprised that he wasn't outside enjoying the mild weather. I found him in the living room, asleep on the sofa. Molly was on the armchair, also asleep.

"Murphy!" I whispered. "Wake up! I've got so much to tell you."

He opened his eyes and was about to smile, then thought better of it.

"Oh. Hello, stranger," he said sleepily, and I noticed Molly's ears flicker. "Where've you been for the last month?"

"Well, it's a long story. My owner put me on Facebook. I've been posting updates. And American cats—they're house cats! And I've set up a blog, too!"

"Nancy, I didn't understand a word of what you just said," he replied, starting to look weary.

"It's all on the computer, Murphy. You should try it—it's so much fun!"

Murphy sighed. "You know I'm not really into computers. Occasionally take naps on the printer, but computers—not so much."

"No, but really, Murphy, it's brilliant. I've got so many new friends!"

His face fell, and then, in silence, he stretched, before walking around the cushion in a slow circle.

Finally, he said, "Good for you," with a voice that was uncharacteristically cold.

I saw Molly's ears flicker again and couldn't resist hissing, "I know you're awake, Molly; you can stop pretending to be asleep," but she remained motionless.

"Come on, Murphy, why don't you give it a try? I could be your first Facebook friend!"

"You're already my friend," he snapped back. "Or at least, I thought you were."

"Of course I'm your friend—Molly, can you please *stop* pretending to be asleep!"

Molly was still curled in a ball, her tail resting on her front paws to hide her face, but I could see that her eyes were open, watching me beadily.

Murphy had settled back down onto his sofa cushion and begun to wash the back of his hind leg, lifting it diagonally so that it obscured his face.

"Fine," I said. "If that's the way you want it."

I jumped down from the sofa and headed for the door.

"I might write about this in my blog, but I guess that won't worry you as you'll never read it," I hissed over my shoulder.

And with that I headed back out through the cat flap, my good mood and optimism thoroughly deflated.

The garden birds had returned from their winter exodus, and they had seemingly forgotten about the existence of cats during their absence.

"What's that?!"

"I think it's a cat!"

"Oh, my god!" they trilled over my head.

"Don't push me," I said out loud. "I'm in a filthy mood right now and killing one of you might just be the only thing that will make me feel better."

That shut them up.

CHAPTER 11

Online Felines

*There's a statistical theory that if you gave
a million cats typewriters and set them to
work, they'd eventually come up with the
complete works of Shakespeare. Thanks to
the Internet, we now know this isn't true.*

—(Adapted from) Ian Hart

It is an indisputable fact that at least 70 percent of content on the Internet is made up of cats, and I soon worked out that these generally fall into three categories.

By far the largest is the "cute home video" category.

These are cats who have been filmed doing something funny: drinking from the toilet, running into a glass door, or cuddling up to a rodent/bird/dog.

Amusing certainly, but not the basis for a media career, I think you'll agree.

The second category is what I call the "techno-gimmick" cats. These are cats who feature in videos cut to music, in which they play the drums, dance on their hind legs, or sing in funny voices.

Now, let's be clear about one thing: these videos fool nobody. We all know that in the close-up shot of the paw holding the drumstick, the paw belongs to a soft toy, not a real cat. The dancing on hind legs is because a human is dangling a feather duster out of the cat's reach. And the funny voices have more to do with a synthesizer program than with the cat itself.

With a cheap piece of home-editing software, a human is able to construct what appears to be a four-minute pop video out of what is actually only three shots. And, like I said, it fools no one.

The third category of cats on the Internet, however, is what can only be described as the "Kitterati." This is an elite band of cats who have a genuine talent and have deservedly hit the big time.

Their skills are varied: some are pianists; some are photographers; some are actors. Others are advice columnists or healers.

These cats, I discovered, don't just have a Facebook page, a blog, or a clip on YouTube. They have their own websites. They have merchandising ranges. They've been on *Oprah*.

And, I realized with a sigh, they were completely out of my league.

I typed in a status update: "Nancy needs to find her USP," and soon I had a dozen thumbs-up, although I noted that none of my friends came up with a suggestion for what my unique selling point could be.

In the absence of an obvious skill on which to build a career, I decided to focus my energies on my blog. I found it surprisingly enjoyable and cathartic to write: it was the perfect way to digest the day-to-day dramas of my life.

Everything from niggling irritations with my owners, or with Pip, to humorous accounts of my adventures around town (the "Nancy set pieces," as I came to think of them), I got it all out of my system through my online diary.

I started to feel like Bridget Jones as I recounted embarrassing yet amusing anecdotes in my journal.*

---

* For the record, if anyone ever decides to make a film out of my memoirs à la Bridget Jones, I will insist on having the deciding vote on

Now that my online friends tally was growing, I had also started to uncover some other British cats on the Internet.

One was a rather exotic-looking cat who sent me a friend request on Facebook. His name was Troy, and in his profile photo he looked like a long-haired Brambles.

I sent him a message:

"Troy's a funny name for such a fancy cat. Are you Siamese?"

A couple of moments later he messaged back:

"No, I'm not Siamese, I'm a chocolate-point Birman. And Troy is short for Troilus Pumpernickel."

I snorted into my laptop. What a great name! And could there really be a breed called "chocolate-point Birman"? It sounded like a snack, not a cat.

"Unusual name," I typed back.

"It's my show name. I'm a Pedigree Grand Master. You can just call me Troy."

Now he had my attention.

"What's a Pedigree Grand Master? And why do you need a show name?"
"For cat shows, of course. Check out my Web site."

So I followed the link he sent to a site detailing the many trophies, rosettes, and awards Troy had won during his career.

———

the actress who is to provide my voice. I'm thinking English rose: a Keira Knightley or an Emily Blunt. Someone with a bit of class, who knows how to speak the Queen's English. No offense, Renée.

There were pages of photos of him next to a grinning woman (his owner, presumably) clutching a garish trophy.

"Liking your bling!" I wrote. "What happens at these shows, exactly?"

"Not a lot, really. You stand on a table, then someone prods you and checks your teeth."

"What, like going to the vet?"

"Not really. It's like a beauty contest. If you win you get a trophy and a check."

This was an interesting concept. I knew the beauty contest thing was dated, and not exactly politically correct, but I did like the sound of the check.

"Could I enter a show?" I asked. "I've got great teeth."

"What breed are you?"

"Er, none that I know of. Hundred percent pure alley cat. Does that count?"

"'Fraid not," he replied. "Shows are for pedigree cats only. Sorry."

This was most frustrating. Here was just the kind of opportunity that would make excellent material for a blog—*the plucky outsider who wowed the judges*, or similar—as well as potentially earning me some money.

So I spent the afternoon surfing cat show websites. There was one coming up in a few days in Birmingham. I scrolled down the list of its categories and classes, amazed that there could be so many breeds of cat that I had never even heard of: Tonkinese, Ocicat, Egyptian Mau.

I finally stumbled upon a "special fun class for nonpedigree cats of traditional moggy appearance."

I must admit I had never particularly thought of myself as a "nonpedigree of traditional moggy appearance" but to hell with that—now was not the time to get bogged down in semantics.

The title was just a long-winded way of saying that anyone could enter.

I sent Troy a message:

> "Troy, guess what. There's a class for moggies at your next show! Can you take me with you?"

> "I don't see why not. You'll have to get over to my house next Wednesday. The show's in Birmingham so we'll need to set off early. Get here by 7 a.m."

He sent me his address, which was in London. I had never been to London before, but I knew where to find my owner's train timetable and A–Z street map, so I was confident that with a bit of planning I would be able to make my own way to Troy's house.

I still had four days to wait until my cat show adventure, but I was dying to tell my news to someone. Murphy was the only member of Team Nancy who might share my excitement, and view the show as an adventure rather than a disaster waiting to happen, but I hadn't seen him since our falling-out over the blog.

In fact, now that I thought about it, I had hardly spent any time with him since New Year's Eve. He had always been the most enthusiastic member of the team, but it was undeniable that recently I had been neglecting him.

In hindsight, it was no wonder that he had been upset when I told him about my new friends on Facebook.

I sighed, accepting the inevitable: I was going to have to apologize.

But it won't hurt to have a nap first, I reasoned, rolling onto my side and resting my head on the keyboard.

When I woke up I could tell from the way my stomach was rumbling that it was nearly dinner time.

I took a detour on the way, via a hedgerow where I knew shrews nested. I picked a plump-looking specimen and dispatched it efficiently with a flick of its neck. Then I carried on to Murphy's house, the shrew hanging from my jaw.

Murphy was asleep on the sofa, in exactly the same spot as the last time I had seen him. The television was on in the background, showing the teatime news.

My parting words from that previous occasion popped into my mind: "I might write about this in my blog, but I guess that won't worry you as you'll never read it." I winced with embarrassment and carefully placed the dead shrew on the carpet in front of the sofa. Murphy was still asleep.

"Murphy," I whispered.

He twitched, startled from a deep sleep, and it took him a couple of moments to notice me.

"Oh, hi," he said, embarrassed at having been caught unawares.

"What's that?" he asked, looking at the shrew.

"A peace offering," I said, pushing the shrew toward him with my paw. "Thought you might be hungry."

"Thanks," he said. "How's the blog?"

I scrutinized his face to see if I could detect any sarcasm in his eyes, but it seemed like a straightforward question.

"It's great, thanks. Look, I'm sorry about . . . everything. I know computers aren't your thing. No more blog talk, I promise."

To my great relief, he smiled.

"That's okay. Shall we?" he asked, gesturing at the shrew.

"After you," I replied. "Age before beauty."

We ate the shrew together, crunching on its bones and depositing the intestines back onto the carpet in the usual manner.

In the background the main news program had finished and the weather forecast was on.

"Listen, I've got a brilliant adventure planned. I'm dying to tell someone about it, if you'd like to hear it."

"Of course," he said. "Go on."

"Well, there are these things called cat shows, and there's a special class—"

I stopped in midsentence, distracted by the television. The local news bulletin had started, and on the screen was a mug shot of a cat: a haggard-looking black-and-white tom with a distinctive scar, looking dolefully into the camera.

"Hang on a minute, Murphy. Can you turn the volume up?" I said urgently.

Murphy obliged, and we watched the news report. The photo had gone from the screen now, replaced by a reporter standing outside a fortresslike building.

"Yes, Graham," the reporter was saying, "staff here at the Shelter for Feral Cats say they have never seen anything like it. Apparently this criminal kitty managed to *dig* his way out through the wall of the shelter, under the very noses of staff and guards." The screen cut to a shot of the wall in question. There was Maud, looking pale and tearful, sliding a cat bed out of the way to reveal a hole in the brickwork, all the way through the external breeze block and out into an alley.

"Oh. My. God," I said, dumbstruck.

"What is it?" asked Murphy, looking alarmed.

"It's Number 29!" I replied. "From the shelter. Do you remember, I told you about him? He's only gone and done it!"

We both looked back at the TV, which now featured the reporter again.

"Staff at the shelter have certainly been given *paws* for thought by this feline runaway. One thing's for sure, Graham," the reporter continued, "this kitty may be gone, but he won't be *fur*gotten."

He delivered this final line with a smile, and Murphy and I both groaned.

"That's pretty cool," said Murphy, turning the volume down.

"It's taken him over two years. That's some serious dedication."

"Don't you mean serious *cat*itude?" Murphy replied.

"I wonder where he'll go," I mused as we jumped off the sofa.

"Who knows? Where would you go if you had escaped?"

"Home, I guess. But he doesn't have one."

We walked through the kitchen together and I was aware of Molly sitting on the dining table, observing us with a look of barely concealed disgust.

"So anyway, let me finish telling you about this show," I continued, and we slipped out through the cat flap into the brisk evening air.

CHAPTER 12

Show Cats

Every cat has beauty, but not everyone sees it.

—(Adapted from) Confucius

I spent the night before the show at home, finalizing my plans for the next day. I had pulled the train timetable out of my owner's handbag and dragged it under the bed to scrutinize its contents.

Could they make those things any more confusing?

"Restrictions apply." . . . "Not valid during peak times."

Fortunately, price plans did not concern me, as I had no intention of paying for a ticket.

I calculated that to get to Troy's place for seven a.m. I would have to be on the 6:15 train. To work out my route from the station to Troy's house I needed the A–Z street map. I climbed onto the desk in the study and attempted to slide it out from underneath a pile of bills, old newspapers, and notepads, inadvertently causing the whole lot to topple onto the floor.

I grabbed the A–Z between my teeth and ran into the bedroom.

Pip had been asleep in the laundry basket and was woken by the commotion. He poked his head out the top of the basket and gave me a quizzical look.

"Oh, it's you. What are you doing there?"

"Nothing," I replied, trying to push the map under the bed with my paw. I had considered telling Pip about my plans, but decided against it, primarily because I couldn't face the inevitable eye rolling and sarcastic comments. He looked as if he was about to challenge me, but then yawned, displaying his enormous white whiskers to their full effect, and disappeared back into the laundry basket.

I squeezed under the bed and opened the A–Z at its index, looking for Troy's street name. Once I had worked out my route I ran back into the study. My owner had returned the pile of papers to its place on the desk and gone downstairs again. The computer was on so I logged on to Facebook and typed a quick message to Troy:

"All systems go! See you tomorrow!"

Then I went into the children's room to settle down for the night.

I woke up at dawn to the birds' chorus of:

"I'm here! Are you still there?"

"Yes, I'm still here!"

"So am I!"

I jumped off the pillow and padded down the stairs. The people were all still asleep and there was no fresh food in the bowl, so I wolfed down the few crunchies left over from the previous night, before briefly checking my reflection in the hallway mirror. Not bad for a nonpedigree of traditional moggy appearance, I thought.

I trotted purposefully out of the house, down the hill, and through the station car park. On the platform I glanced at the notice board and was relieved to see that my train was running on time. There were a few commuters standing around, but they all had the same glazed expression on their faces and didn't even seem to notice each other, let alone me.

When the train arrived I ran down to the last car and as the doors slid open I jumped in, climbing into a crevice between some seats that was intended for luggage. There was a heater blowing warm air behind me so I had to concentrate on not falling asleep—I could not afford to miss my stop.

As we approached my destination, the train slowed to a halt on the tracks and I could hear some of the other passengers tutting. After a couple of moments the driver's voice crackled through the intercom: "I'd like to apologize to customers for the delay in this service. It has been caused by a signal failure on the line ahead. We'll be on our way as quickly as possible."

This prompted even more tutting from the passengers, and my heart started to race. Signal failure was definitely *not* something I had allowed for in my itinerary. I sat in my luggage crevice, fuming.

How was a cat supposed to build a career when public transport could not be relied upon? Some of us had work to do. Was it really so hard for the train company to do its job properly?

I began composing my e-mail of complaint when suddenly the train jolted into life again. It crawled at barely walking speed for the last hundred yards of the journey, until I finally saw the station signs slide past the window opposite me, and I breathed a sigh of relief.

The doors opened and I darted across the platform and onto the street.

Once out of the station I knew the next part of the journey would be easy. I had memorized my route from the A–Z and, besides, it's true what they say about cats having an innate sense of direction.

In five minutes I had reached Troy's road, and immediately I noticed a car with its trunk open, into which a cat basket was being placed. I ran toward the car, and when Troy's owner went to lock up the house, I put my front paws up on the rear bumper.

"Troy? Is that you?" I whispered.

"Yes," he replied. "Quick, jump in."

I leapt in and hid among the coats, shopping bags, and umbrellas people always seem to store in the trunk of their car. A moment later the owner reappeared and slammed the door shut.

The engine started, the car pulled away, and we were off! I crawled out from under the coats and walked to the front of Troy's cat box.

"Hi, Troy. I'm Nancy. Pleased to meet you."

I had never seen such a well-groomed feline. He was indeed like a fluffier version of Brambles, except that his long fur had been combed and teased to perfection, and his eyes were implausibly blue. He had competed in shows all his life, I learned, as his owner was a breeder.

"What do you do when you're not at a show?" I asked.

"Not a lot, really. I go to the groomer's. I sleep. Facebook's my savior, really."

"I know that feeling."

"And I've got an irritable bowel so I have to follow a strict diet. I've got a nutrition chart to fill in."

"Of course," I said, trying to suppress a smile.

After a while the movement of the car and noise of the engine had us both nodding off. Troy rummaged at the back of his cat box and pulled out a satin eye mask and pair of fluffy earmuffs. As he pulled the mask over his eyes he looked at me apologetically.

"Sorry, I haven't got a spare."

"Don't worry, I'm fine," I replied, and I curled up on the coats and allowed myself to drift into sleep.

I woke up as soon as the engine was switched off, and I quickly dived under the coats to hide. As Troy's owner lifted the cat box out and looked in her bag for her paperwork, I jumped down and hid under the car.

So this was Birmingham. From where I was standing, Birmingham appeared to be a huge parking lot. A large building loomed ahead of us, with "NEC" written above the entrance.

As Troy's owner picked up the cat box and set off toward the building, I followed, sticking close to other cars so as not to draw attention to myself. I slipped through the sliding doors behind a group of people and found myself inside an enormous exhibition hall.

Reader, I had never seen anything like it in my life.

Everywhere I looked there were owners clutching cat boxes, standing in queues waiting to register their pets. I heard a few yowls mixed with the hubbub of human voices, from cats who were either unfamiliar with the show environment or overexcited about what was to come.

Troy's owner had joined a queue where an usher was shouting:

"Chocolate- and cream-point Birmans over here, please."

"Good luck!" I called to Troy before setting off to look for my own class.

I was amazed by the variety of cats in the hall. Some of them were downright freaky looking.

There were cats with no fur, who were crouched in their carriers, shivering. There were cats with giant ears, or ears that seemed to have been folded over at the tips, as if a window had been slammed shut on them.

One of the cats I passed had no tail.

"What happened to your tail?" I asked, shocked. "Did you have an accident?"

The cat looked at me with disdain.

"No, of courth I did not have an accthident. I am a Mankth cat. It hath taken yearth of inbreeding to cultivate my tail-lethneth."

"Oh, okay, sorry," I replied. I nearly added, "Did it take yearth of inbreeding to cultivate your lithp, too?" but I bit my tongue.

In addition to the lisp I noticed that this cat also had a squint, and I couldn't help wondering whether the years of inbreeding had been a good thing.

Class 32 was for blue and lilac Persians. Something about the Persians' wide, flat faces and squashed noses made me want to laugh, they just looked so—stupid.

They all seemed to know each other and were evidently seasoned show cats. As I walked past their carriers I could hear their snuffly breathing, in spite of all the background noise in the hall. They were making snide remarks to each other.

"Who's done your fur this time? It looks . . . different."

"Have you changed your diet? You're looking . . . voluptuous."

I couldn't resist peering inside their boxes to get a closer look.

"Who are *you*?" one of them asked dismissively.

"I'm Nancy. I'm entering the moggy class. Just thought I'd have a look around first."

"Good luck," one of them said. "I think you'll need it."

Eventually I came across the "special fun class"—class number 58. Finally, here were some cats who looked . . . well, like cats. A hodgepodge collection of moggies like you would find on any street.

The class was due to begin shortly and the owners were getting the cats out of their carriers in preparation. I spotted a friendly-looking marmalade tom and hopped up onto the table next to him.

"Hi, I'm Nancy," I said.

"I'm Dave."

"What's that short for?" I asked, expecting to hear a convoluted show name: Davidius Pipistrelli or something equally whimsical.

"It's short for Dave."

"Oh," I said, sheepishly.

"You haven't been to one of these before, have you?" he added.

"Is it that obvious?"

He smiled.

"Are you a Grand Master?" I asked.

"Of course not. Only a pedigree can be a Grand Master. My

stepcat is a Grand Master. She's Bengal. I just get dragged around these shows to keep her company."

"Oh, right," I replied. "Do you enjoy them?"

"Honestly? Not really. You spend hours in the car, then ages in your carrier waiting for your class. You get prodded and peered at for five minutes, and then it's back in your car for the journey home. Trust me, it's not what it's cracked up to be."

"Don't you get a check if you win?"

"No, your owner gets a check. You get a ribbon."

"Oh," I said, feeling a little disappointed.

There was an awkward silence as Dave contemplated his surroundings with evident ennui.

Just then a group of people arrived at our area and the mood changed among the owners (although less so among the moggies, most of whom, it seemed, couldn't care less). I deduced from the air of excitement that this huddle of people must be the judges, and that our class was about to begin.

I sat patiently next to Dave on his table, trying my hardest to look like I was meant to be there. An usher walked past me shouting, "Whose is this cat? Can the owner of this cat please come and find me!" but I pretended not to understand.

When the judges reached our table I let Dave go first, watching with admiration as he allowed them to manipulate his body into certain positions, poke around in his mouth, and pull out his tail. I had to admit it wasn't the most dignified procedure.

Then it was my turn. I played willing as the judges examined me, but if I'm honest it was a somewhat degrading experience. The judges didn't once look me in the eye, and the way they moved my body around made me feel like a piece of meat. I could hear them muttering among themselves, "Where has this one come from? I'm not sure she's even registered to enter."

"I can hear you, you know," I meowed at them. "And, for the record, I do have a brain, too."

My chances of winning were looking slim. It hadn't occurred to me until now that I might lose on a bureaucratic technicality.

It was a surprisingly fast process, as the judges made their way around the tables and performed the same perfunctory assessment of all the entrants.

I had been expecting some Oscars-style announcement of the winner from a gold envelope, but instead one of the judges, an elderly lady who looked as if she would rather be at home watching *Antiques Roadshow*, called out, "Number twelve," and all eyes turned to my table.

For a fleeting moment I thought I had won, but then I heard Dave's owner scream. He had taken the top spot.

The judge called out the numbers of the runners-up and I realized that I had not ranked.

Dave's owner rushed forward to collect his ribbon and trophy, and of course her check, and then ran back to our table to attach the huge pink ribbon to Dave's collar. There was muted applause among the rest of the owners as the show photographer came and took their picture.

Dave cast me a look while this was going on, as if to say "See what I mean?" and, I had to admit, he had a point.

I could tell the show was winding up, as everywhere I looked there were owners clutching trophies, and cats wearing improbably large rosettes. I made my way back to Troy's class, and as I reached the Persians, I could hear them hissing at each other.

"I think the judges need to get their eyes tested. I can see your cellulite from here," said one, who was wearing a modest "3rd Place" ribbon.

"Shut it, bitch. You're just jealous," replied another, caressing her huge pink winner's bow.

"Now, now, girls, it's not the winning that counts, but the taking part," I called out as I walked past.

I arrived at Troy's area in time to see him posing for a photo—true to form he had ranked first in his class.

As he climbed back into his cat box I congratulated him on his win.

"Thanks very much. Another one to add to the collection," he said, although I thought his voice lacked conviction.

It was gone nine p.m. by the time I finally slipped through the cat flap at NHQ, and I felt shattered. After the drive back from Birmingham I had ended up caught in the evening rush hour. My train home from London had been late, and it was packed with irate commuters. I had endured much tutting, not to mention a bruised tail where a bad-tempered man "accidentally" trod on me as I tried to make my way past him to the luggage crevice.

I dragged myself up the hill from the station and, once back at NHQ, went straight to the sofa to wash and reflect on the day's events. I was in no doubt that being a show cat would not suit me as a career. It seemed to me that the shows existed for the enjoyment of the owners, rather than the cats. Even the winners had seemed to find victory a fairly hollow experience.

Besides, I was a modern cat and I wanted a modern career: one in which success would depend upon my talent, not my looks.

I knew I could do better than this.

CHAPTER 13

Would Like to Meet

Youth is easily deceived because it is quick to hope.

—Aristotle

I was flicking through a celebrity gossip magazine one morning, looking for my favorite feature: "Ugh! How could they leave the house looking like that?"

The magazine's highlight, this was a photo spread of human celebrities in varying states of wardrobe malfunction.

As was often the case, I had no idea who most of the "celebrities" were. It seemed that many of them had achieved fame without doing much to merit it. A reality show here, a sex tape there—it didn't take a lot to become a human celebrity, apparently.

I sighed, wondering why the same rules didn't apply for cats.

Beginning to lose interest, I skimmed through the rest of the magazine, only stopping when I stumbled across an advertising promotion for none other than Kit-e-Licious cat food.

The full-page advert showed the Kit-e-Licious cat on his hind legs, emerging from the sea onto a white sandy beach. He was wearing a pair of tight-fitting, light blue swimming trunks, and his muscles rippled under his glistening fur. The overall look was not unlike Daniel Craig in *Casino Royale* (apart from the fur, obviously).

On the beach were clusters of sun loungers, on which female cats reclined. Some were wearing sunglasses, which they had tipped forward to give themselves a better view; others were holding cocktails, which had started to spill.

They all stared slack jawed at Mr. Kit-e-Licious, whose amber-green eyes gazed straight into the camera with a look that could only be described as devastatingly attractive.

"Is my body too Kit-e-Licious for *you*?" ran the tagline across the bottom of the page.

"Absolutely *not!*" I giggled.

Naturally I then did what any computer-savvy cat with nothing planned for the day would do. I ran upstairs, logged on to the computer, and searched Google for "Kit-e-Licious cat + blue trunks."

Surely he's got to be on here somewhere, I figured.

My heart leapt when, less than a second later, over three thousand results flashed up on-screen. Mostly they were links to chat forums where feline fans could post their appreciative, and sometimes rather explicit, comments:

"OMG this cat is SO HOT!!! Purr purr," wrote one of the more demure contributors.

I typed into the search bar, "Who is Kit-e-Licious cat," and several thousand more pages appeared.

I scanned the results, but the upshot was, no one knew who he was. This cat's true identity was a closely guarded secret.

My eyes were drawn to the sidebar of the website, where a stream of advertisements flickered.

The first was an advert for feline Viagra: "For the Alpha male who likes to be *up* all night."

The second was an advice helpline for cats: "Antisocial Siamese? Paranoid Persian? Bulimic Burmese? Whatever your pedigree problem—call our confidential helpline now."

The third was for a feline dating website. "Looking for Mr. Right? Look no further than Datemycat.com" flashed the slogan, over a picture of two cats in a cozy embrace.

I could not resist the impulse to click on the link. What did I have to lose?

The website's home page popped up on screen, boasting of its success in finding love for its members. I looked through some of the user profiles. A few were house cats looking for on-line pen friends. Another was a female whose kittens had finally been homed and who was raring to "get her life back." They seemed to be a pretty normal bunch.

Why not, I thought, and I clicked on the "sign up" tab.

"Choose your user name," the website prompted.

I thought for a few minutes before typing "Molly."

In the "Interests" category I highlighted "Internet/blogging," "hunting/fishing," and "travel/sightseeing." Then I reread the list and added "politics/current affairs," thinking it might help to weed out some of the less intelligent users.

I filled in the "About Me" box with two hundred carefully chosen words and clicked "submit."

The deed was done. My profile would go live on the site the next day.

I leaned back from the keyboard and turned round to see Pip sitting on the landing, evidently watching what I was doing. I hurriedly closed the Datemycat.com page as he said, "What *are* you up to now?" with a tone of exaggerated weariness.

"Nothing. Besides, it's none of your business anyway."

I jumped down from the desk and strolled past him, refusing to meet his gaze.

The following morning when I logged on to the computer, there was a message from Datemycat.com.

"You have been contacted by 2 members!" the e-mail announced.

Jolly good, I thought.

The first message was from "Politicat," an eight-year-old tom whose owner was an MP. He wrote that he would love to get to know me better and hoped we could share some lively political debates.

Meh, I thought. Political debates weren't really what I had in mind.

I closed Politicat's message, eager to see who my other respondent was.

This was a cat whose user name was BigStuff. His message read:

> "Hi. You seem like a fun cat. I think we've got lots in common. I travel for work so I use the Internet a lot. I'd love to read your blog some time."

This sounded promising. The allusion to travel and work intrigued me: clearly this cat had an interesting life. And of course the request to read my blog flattered my vanity. I replied to Politicat first, saying it must be interesting to live with a politician (I lied) and that it would be nice to find out more about him.

Then I replied to BigStuff, asking what he did as a career and sending him a link to my blog.

For the rest of the day I resisted the urge to check the computer.

I'll check my e-mails at two p.m., I thought—not a second sooner.

I ate a few mouthfuls of food, had a perfunctory wash, and tried to nap. When the time came, I walked casually past Pip on his radiator hammock and sauntered upstairs to the study. I broke into a smile upon seeing an e-mail from Datemycat.com, saying I had two messages.

I opened Politicat's first. He wrote that he lived in the countryside and was the only cat of the household. He sometimes felt lonely, as his owner often went away for work. He ended by saying that he would love to find out a bit more about me and hoped we could meet up in due course.

Maybe I had been a bit hard on him initially. He came across as a thoughtful cat, and at least he hadn't mentioned the political debate thing again. I felt sorry for him and his lonely lifestyle, so I composed a charming but noncommittal reply.

Then I opened BigStuff's message, which began, "I *love* your blog!" He praised my writing style and sense of humor, even quoting a couple of his favorite lines.

He said he couldn't tell me any details about his career, as he was meant to keep his identity a secret, but he was in show business and was often required to travel for his assignments.

Reader, I'm sure you can guess what went through my mind. *Could BigStuff be the Kit-e-Licious cat?*

My heart began to race, and I typed back:

"Have you been to any exotic beaches recently? And do you own blue swimming trunks?"

Surely it couldn't be this easy to track down the elusive Mr. Kit-e-Licious. But, then, maybe it was fate—perhaps we were meant to find each other. My tail twitched with excitement.

After about twenty minutes there was a flicker on the screen as a new message appeared in my in-box. "BigStuff has sent you a message," it read. I took a deep breath and clicked "open."

"I did have one assignment on a beach in Bali recently, but don't tell anyone I told you that.

"Blue swimming trunks? That's for me to know, and you to find out ;-)

"P.S. While we're on the subject of clothes, what are you wearing right now?"

I gasped in disbelief. Bali. Where was Bali? Did it have white sandy beaches? I had to know, *now*.

I opened up Google and typed in "Bali + beaches," then, as an afterthought, added "+ kit-e-licious." Almost instantly, a list of pages appeared, the first of which was titled "The beach from the Kit-e-Licious advert." In the paragraph underneath I could see that, yes, the "blue swimming trunks" photo had been shot on location in Bali. Surely there was only one explanation: BigStuff and Mr. Kit-e-Licious were one and the same cat!

I closed down the Google results page and reread his message. The more I read it, the more convinced I became. Surely it was unlikely that another cat in show business had been to Bali. And his comment about the blue swimming trunks implied that he did indeed own some.

Then I reread the P.S., in which he asked what I was wearing. I had been so excited that I had hardly noticed it before. Why did he want to know what *I* was wearing?

I opened up a new message.

"When you say you're in show business, do you mean you're an actor? And if so, have you ever been in a cat food commercial?

"P.S. I'm just wearing my usual collar. It's kind of glittery gold, and fraying a bit at the edges."

Within thirty seconds a reply appeared:

"If I told you that, I'd have to kill you ;-)

"P.S. Why don't you take your collar off?"

Reader, I'll be honest with you, this reply troubled me.

I was more certain than ever that I was corresponding with Mr. Kit-e-Licious, but why all the interest in my collar?

Part of me wanted to arrange a meeting so I could find out

his identity once and for all. But another part of me was urging caution, telling me that something wasn't quite right.

"When in doubt, wash," said my mother's voice again, and while I washed, I thought.

What did I know *for sure* about this cat? He said he was in show business and that he had been to Bali. He had not definitively said that he was an actor or that he owned blue swimming trunks, but he had *implied* both. And he said he had to keep his identity secret for work, something that I knew was true of the Kit-e-Licious star. There were too many similarities for it to be a coincidence, weren't there?

Or perhaps it was too much of a coincidence.

There was no obligation to tell the truth on the website, I acknowledged, looking again at my profile under the name "Molly."

And if he wasn't Mr. Kit-e-Licious, who was he?

Finishing my wash, I knew I could not ignore my instinct that something was amiss.

Just then the doorbell rang, and my heart froze. It couldn't be him, could it? It suddenly occurred to me that he had read my blog and would have been able to work out where I lived from that.

I heard my owner walking down the hall toward the front door and held my breath.

"Sorry to trouble you, madam. I'm from the police—Online Vice Squad. Has anyone in this house been using a website called Datemycat.com?"

"A website called *what?*" my owner replied.

I couldn't see from the landing, but I could imagine the appalled look on her face. It was a look I had seen many times before.

"Datemycat.com," the police officer repeated. "It's a dating website . . . for cats."

At this point Pip emerged from the bedroom and sat about two feet away, staring at me.

"A dating website for cats?" My owner laughed. "Of course

not! Why would we . . . oh, hang on a minute. *Nancy!*" she shouted up the stairs, any trace of laughter gone from her voice.

I ran into the study and hid behind the door, cringing as I heard my owner invite the policeman into the house.

He explained that they had been tracking activity on the Date My Cat site for several months, as there had been reports of a human "cat fetishist" masquerading as a cat.

"I'm sorry, a human *what?*" my owner asked.

"An adult male . . . human, who poses as a . . . feline to gain the trust of female cats. Once he has established contact he then begins"—the policeman lowered his voice—"to *groom* them."

Groom them for what, I thought—a cat show?

My owner paused, in evident disbelief, before saying, "Oh, *yuck!*"

"We've been monitoring the suspect for some time, madam, and we have reason to believe he may have entered into a correspondence with a . . . cat in this household."

"Oh, God," said my owner. "Well, we've got two cats, but I think I know which one you're talking about. Do you know who this man is?"

"We do now, madam. We were waiting for him to strike again, and thanks to your cat, we've caught him red-handed. He won't be passing himself off as a feline anymore. We just wanted to let you know in person. And it might be a good idea to give your cat one of these, if she spends a lot of time on the computer."

He handed something to my owner, then she thanked him and showed him to the door, and he left.

I heard her stomping up the stairs, and Pip instantly darted into the bedroom.

"Nancy! Where are you?" she shouted.

She marched into the study and swung the door shut, revealing me pressed up against the baseboard.

"The police? Well, this is a new one! Quite an achievement, even for you!"

I cowered, trying to hide behind the computer modem,

which sat on the floor by the door. I noticed, for the first time, that it emitted a high-pitched whistling noise that was most unpleasant at close proximity.

"Fortunately the police have caught this . . . cat fetishist . . . weirdo, before he came to find you. Please, no more dating sites in future!" And with that she threw a leaflet down onto the floor in front of me before storming back down the stairs.

"Keeping Safe Online: A Guide for Your Feline" it was called.

"It's a bit late for that, don't you think?" I shouted after her, but she didn't hear me.

I closed my eyes and took a deep breath.

What a total, unmitigated disaster. How was I supposed to know there were such things as "cat fetishists"? What kind of human freak got his kicks from chatting up cats on a dating website?

But how stupid had I been to fall for his patter about show business and Bali? He must have used the same line on dozens of other cats, all of whom were probably as eager as I was to believe he was Mr. Kit-e-Licious.

I logged on to the computer to delete BigStuff from my "Friends" folder, but I didn't need to. He had already been removed from the site, and aside from the humiliating e-mails in my in-box there was no evidence that he had ever existed. I sighed, still reeling with shame from the whole sorry episode.

"You have 1 new message," read a window on the screen. My heart lurched—he couldn't still be able to contact me, could he?

I breathed a sigh of relief when I saw that the message was from Politicat.

To whoever you are,

Please leave Politicat alone. Whatever he told you, he is not an only cat. He has a wife, and I am she. You are not the first cat he has tried this with, and I daresay you won't be the last, but trust me, he's not worth it. He's overweight, he's a liar, and he's useless in the sack.

From,

Mrs. Politicat

I groaned and deleted the message. Then I went into the "My Account" page of the Date My Cat website and clicked on "remove my profile."

"Are you sure you want to permanently delete your profile?" the site asked.

"Hell, yeah," I said as I clicked on "yes."

CHAPTER 14

Nancy's Got Talent

*Everybody has talent, it's just a matter of
moving around until you've discovered what
it is.*

—George Lucas

I sat at the computer, disappointed and humiliated. How ridiculous to think that I could stumble across the Kit-e-Licious cat on a dating website. Of course he wouldn't use such sites. He was a celebrity: he could have his pick of any female cat he wanted. Another one to chalk up to experience, I concluded with a sigh.

I stared out the window at the garden, wondering whether to head out and find Team Nancy or just curl up on the keyboard and go to sleep.

My eye was caught by a movement at the bottom of the garden—a fleeting glimpse of a black-and-white cat in the undergrowth.

That's weird, I thought, I hadn't heard Pip leave the bedroom.

I jumped down from the desk, walked up to the laundry basket, and poked at its lumpy contents with my paw. Sure enough, Pip's claws immediately pierced the fabric where my paw had touched.

"*What* do you think you're doing? I'm trying to sleep in here."

"Sorry, Pip. Just checking."

Could there be a new black-and-white cat in the neighborhood? This was the first I'd heard of it.

I went into the garden, but there was no sign of the cat now. Oh, well, I thought, heading in the direction of Murphy's house. I knew that if anyone would be able to make me forget about the day's dramas, it would be him.

I arrived as he and Molly were finishing their dinner.

"Hiya," he mumbled through a mouthful of Kit-e-Licious.

"Evening," I replied. "Fancy hanging out tonight?"

"Sure. What do you want to do?"

"Don't know, really. I kind of feel like staying in. Is that okay?"

"No problem," he replied. "*Britain's Got Talent*'s about to start—we can laugh at all the weirdos!"

I winced at his use of the word "weirdos," but said, "Great idea," and we settled down side by side on the sofa.

I had seen *Britain's Got Talent* a few times before, and I knew the format. It was the auditions stage, and the bulk of the show was taken up with an assortment of oddballs performing acts that were unremittingly awful. Murphy got into the spirit of things, shouting, "Off! Off! Off!" with the live audience at the worst offenders.

As the show neared its end, überjudge Simon Cowell was interviewed backstage. "I don't think we've ever seen such dreadful auditions. I'm really worried about the quality of this year's contestants."

Murphy turned to me with a knowing look. "He *always* says that when someone good's about to come on. Just wait and see!"

Next up was a middle-aged woman accompanied by her dog, a border collie. Murphy and I looked at each other, perplexed.

"A dog? Dogs don't have talent!" I said and he shrugged.

A big band classic struck up and the woman and her dog

began a dance routine, in which he slalomed between her legs, walked backward in circles, and lifted alternate paws in time to the music. It ended with the dog standing on his hind legs, his front paws resting on her backside. His eyes looked crazed with excitement, he was panting, and his tongue was hanging out.

I snorted with derision, waiting for the audience to start chanting, but instead they erupted into cheers. I watched in disbelief as the judges commented on the performance.

Piers Morgan said the act was "exactly what this show needs."

The blond woman in the middle was moved to tears.

"Come on, Simon, talk some sense into them," I muttered. But no, Simon Cowell was touched by their "special relationship."

There was a tense silence as the judges pondered their verdict, and the screen cut to the audience, hands over their mouths in anticipation. . . .

The dancing dog had three yeses and was through to the finals! The crowd were on their feet, cheering. The dog leapt up into his owner's arms. The blond judge in the middle started crying again.

The credits began to roll and Murphy and I stared at each other, openmouthed.

"What just happened there?" I asked.

Had I imagined it, or had a dog just gone onstage, run in circles with its tongue hanging out, and somehow won the nation's hearts, potentially launching a media career in the process?

"That's ridiculous!" I said and Murphy nodded in agreement.

"I've got more talent in the tip of my tail than that dog has in his whole body!"

"You don't dance, do you?"

"Well, no. But I can sing better than he can dance!"

Murphy's eyes lit up.

"Hang on a minute." He jumped down from the sofa and ran across the room to the CD player. He pressed play, and Celine Dion warbled out of the speakers. I grimaced.

"I can't sing to *that*."

Murphy began fiddling with the machine.

"I've got just the song for you!" He smiled and inserted a new CD. It was a song I was familiar with from the little people's music collection: "Beautiful" by Christina Aguilera. This was a song I could work with. *Britain's Got Talent* had never showcased a feline diva, and it was about time that changed. My voice was a little croaky at first, and I struggled to remember the lyrics, pick up the melody, and inject emotion into my performance all at the same time.

When I had finished I looked nervously at Murphy to gauge his reaction. He paused for a second before applauding wildly.

"Wonderful!" he exclaimed.

"Really? You're not just saying that?"

"Really. Might need a bit of practice, in parts, but it's the perfect song for you."

If Murphy's response was anything to go by, maybe my USP had been staring me in the face all along. For months I had been searching for something to mark me out from other cats but had overlooked my god-given talent: my voice.

Over the next few days I threw myself into my new vocation, taking every opportunity to practice. I sang while I washed, to much eye rolling from Pip. I sang as I did my daily rounds of the gardens. I sang from the moment I woke up until the moment I went to sleep (which, admittedly, was sometimes only an hour after I had woken up).

But if I was serious about entering *Britain's Got Talent*, I knew I needed to re-create the show's audition conditions.

"Murphy, I need your help!" I called through his cat flap one afternoon, and he duly emerged from the kitchen. He followed me down the garden, and I left him sitting on the footpath behind NHQ.

"You're going to be Simon Cowell. Wait here while I go and recruit the other two."

I returned ten minutes later with Bella and Brambles, both of whom were nervous, unsure what was expected of them.

I lined the three of them up on the path.

"Bella, you're in the middle; you're the blond one. Try and look . . . blond."

Bella looked at me blankly.

"That's perfect, Bella. Well done."

I turned to Brambles.

"Brambles, you're Piers Morgan."

"I'm sorry—I'm *who*?" Brambles interrupted, the panic visible in his eyes.

"Doesn't matter. Just sit there and look . . . smug. Murphy's going to be Simon Cowell."

I stepped back to assess them.

"Right, that'll have to do. I'm going to hide behind this tree and then walk out here to the stage"—I glanced at them— "and please try not to look so much like the Three Stooges."

They composed themselves.

"Okay, are you all ready?"

They nodded, and I went and hid behind the tree.

I took a deep breath, then walked out to the middle of the path. They stared at me in silence.

"Well, ask me a few questions!" I hissed.

"Who's Piers Morgan?" Brambles said. I shot him a dirty look.

"Questions *about me*, Brambles!"

"Oh, sorry," Brambles replied, falling silent again.

"How much do you want to be a singer?" Murphy shouted.

"One hundred ten percent, Simon," I replied, giving Murphy a big smile.

"What are you going to sing?" Bella ventured timidly.

"Well . . . blond one . . . I'm going to sing the classic ballad by Christina Aguilera: 'Beautiful.'"

"We're ready when you are," said Brambles, finally starting to get the hang of it.

I have to admit I felt genuinely nervous, and my nerves were not helped by hearing the birds in the surrounding trees head for the sky as I started singing. But I kept my performance on track, and as the song drew to a close Murphy rose to his feet to give me a standing ovation. My face broke into a big smile, and I looked across at the judges.

"Well, what did you all think?" I asked.

"Amazing," said Murphy.

"Why, thank you, Simon!" I replied coquettishly, and he winked at me.

I looked at Bella. Her eyes were brimming with tears.

"Blimey, Bella. You really *are* like the blond one in the middle! Did you like it?"

She nodded, wiping her eyes. I knew I was unlikely to get a rational response from her so I turned to Brambles.

"Well, what did you think, Piers?"

Brambles wrinkled his nose thoughtfully.

"Honestly? I think the overall effect was . . . like a drunken aunt at a wedding."

There was a tense silence as Murphy and Bella stared at him in shock. I narrowed my eyes.

"Brambles. You're meant to be Piers Morgan. Not Simon Cowell. Let's try that again."

Brambles looked suitably shamefaced and closed his eyes to think for a few moments.

"In that case, I think you're exactly what this show needs!"

"Much better. Thank you, Piers."

I took a big stretch, then said, "Good work, team. You're free to go."

A little later, I was sitting at the bottom of my garden, tuning up for my last rehearsal of the day, when I heard another cat yowling in the distance.

"Do you mind?" I called. "This isn't a duet!" The yowling stopped.

It was a balmy early summer's evening and there was no one around, apart from a neighbor watering his garden.

It felt good, finally to know what my true calling was.

Channeling my inner Aguilera, I closed my eyes and began to sing, my vocals soaring as I reached the first chorus.

Christina's right, I thought, as I belted out the lyrics: I *am* beautiful!

Suddenly I felt the force of a jet of cold water on my back. I turned to see the neighbor pointing his garden hose over the fence at me, a vindictive grin on his face. Furious, I ran across the lawn and into the house.

The philistine! How dare he?

It took me a good half hour to lick the water off, during which time I heard the neighbor talking to my owner over the fence. I heard him use the words "never heard meowing like it" and "please make her stop."

A few moments later when my owner came in, I pretended to be asleep.

"No more singing, Nancy. Please." And she walked off.

Yet again, my ambitions had been thwarted by small-minded people who didn't have an ounce of talent in their bodies. If I couldn't practice, there was no way I could audition for *Britain's Got Talent*. And if I couldn't get on *Britain's Got Talent*, how would I ever become famous and meet Mr. Kit-e-Licious?

Was I ever going to get the break I deserved?

I slumped on the sofa in despair.

Then again, I concluded, maybe it was for the best. I couldn't ignore the fact that, apart from Murphy, no one had outright complimented me on my singing. And did I really want to risk the jeers of a live audience and humiliation in front of the nation if the judges didn't like me? In hindsight, perhaps this particular plan had not been one of my better ideas. Even if I had given it 110 percent.

I had a nap, and when I woke I felt refreshed and surprisingly optimistic.

When one door closes, another one opens, I figured, and I would just have to keep looking till I found the right door.

I jumped down from the sofa and headed out onto the street. I had not visited the corner shop for some time, and I felt a hankering for their fresh ham. I trotted through the open door and chirruped hello to the girl behind the counter. True to form, she picked up a few scraps of ham and put them on the floor for me.

As I was leaving the shop I noticed a poster pinned to the notice board.

"Auditions: this weekend!" it announced. The Smalltown Players (the town's amateur dramatics society) was planning to stage a "groundbreaking adaptation" of George Orwell's *Animal Farm* and would be holding open auditions on Saturday.

"Everyone welcome: even animals!" read the poster.

Could this be right? A drama society inviting animals to audition for a play? Surely this must be the door I was looking for.

CHAPTER 15

The Show Must Go On

All cats are equal, but some are more equal than others.

—(Adapted from) George Orwell

At the appointed time on Saturday I made my way to the church hall where the *Animal Farm* auditions were being held. I could hear the hubbub of chat and laughter inside, and my stomach lurched in anticipation. It crossed my mind, as I hovered outside the door, that aside from my mock audition in front of Team Nancy, I had never actually performed for anyone before.

I slipped into the hall and looked around. There were a couple dozen people milling about, clutching biscuits and plastic cups of tea. I was somewhat underwhelmed by the group, which seemed mostly comprised of middle-aged housewives and men who probably used to be accountants but had long since retired.

One woman had brought along an overweight golden retriever, who lay at her feet licking biscuit crumbs off the floor while she chatted. Apart from the dog, I couldn't see any other animal auditioners.

Observing the room from my place by the door, I spotted a man whom I deduced was the show's director. He was, like nearly everyone else in the room, on the wrong side of middle age. As well as being almost completely bald, he had a physique that betrayed a love of rich food. The only thing that marked him out from the rest of the throng was a silk neckerchief at the collar of his shirt, and a pair of red-rimmed glasses, which he would theatrically sweep off his face and gesticulate with when talking.

After about ten minutes of chat, the director jumped (or rather, belly flopped and scrambled) onto the stage.

"Can I have everyone's attention, please?"

The room quieted.

"Thank you all very much for coming. I'm Quentin and I'll be directing this stage adaptation of *Animal Farm*. It's lovely to see so many familiar faces, but it's also fabulous to see some *un*familiar faces, too. I'm referring especially to our *animal* auditioners."

At this there was a murmur of laughter and a few "awwws" as the others looked at me and at the retriever, who was working his way across the floor, systematically vacuuming up crumbs.

"I'm *rather* excited about this," Quentin went on. "No one has ever staged this play using a combined human *and* animal cast. It's going to be a truly groundbreaking production and a totally immersive audience experience."

He paused, waiting for a reaction. Someone called out a half-hearted, "Hear! Hear!" and Quentin smiled and bowed his head.

"So, without further ado, let the auditions commence!" he announced with a final flourish of his glasses.

I moved forward from my position by the door and jumped up onto a pile of tables stacked at the side of the room. The auditioners took turns reading a passage of text from the script, after which Quentin, rather indiscriminately, I thought, lavished praise on them: "Beautiful, darling. You moved me to tears!"

When the human auditions were finished, Quentin said, "Thank you, everybody. There were some really exciting auditions and I'll announce the parts next week. However, there are a couple of roles I can cast today, and I think you can probably guess which parts I'm talking about."

He cast a sly grin in my direction.

All eyes turned to me and the dog, who was now asleep underneath my table.

"Ladies and gentlemen, can I please introduce you to . . ." He fumbled with my name tag. ". . . Nancy, who will be playing the Cat, and to Toffy, who will be playing the Dog."

There was a cheer and more "awwws."

"Thank you, everyone," Quentin shouted over the melee. "Please come back same time next week, when I'll be handing out scripts."

The auditioners started to disperse, several of them stroking me on their way out. One man said, "Well, Nancy. I daresay you'll be *purr*-fect for the role," much to his own amusement.

"Very good. You should be a journalist," I shot back, but he couldn't hear me over the sound of his own laughter.

Is that it? I thought, when everyone had gone.

I was rather disappointed that I had not been asked to audition like everyone else. Although, given that no other cats had turned up, it was not as if I had any competition.

I jumped down from my table and made my way outside. It was a glorious sunny day and as I walked home I began to feel rather excited about my forthcoming stage debut.

If Toffy the retriever was to be the only other animal cast member, I felt confident that I would shine onstage. And who knew where this foray into acting might lead? The local press would no doubt come to review the opening night, and there might even be talent scouts in the audience. This could be the start of a whole new career.

At home I headed upstairs to the little people's bedroom and jumped onto one of the beds. An innate professional, I knew it was important that I get enough sleep. I curled up in a ball and was soon dreaming of the show's first night, in which a certain famous cat sat in the front row, applauding my performance.

The following Saturday, I made my way again to the church hall for rehearsals and sat patiently as Quentin announced the parts for the human cast. He started with the main parts, the pigs. Why the author had chosen to make all his main characters porcine was a mystery to me. Don't get me wrong, pigs are intelligent animals, but they are totally uncivilized and definitely *not* natural leaders in the animal kingdom. There were also lesser parts for horses, a pony, some sheep, and a few human characters, too. Being a perceptive feline, I could sense envy among some of the players as the main parts were announced. Toffy and I sat side by side, observing proceedings.

"Have you been in one of these plays before?" I asked.

"Huh? Nope. I'm only here for the biscuits," he replied before flopping onto the parquet floor and closing his eyes.

Once Quentin had read out the cast list and handed round scripts, he gave us some background about the play. *Animal Farm*, he explained, was Orwell's satirical fable on the development of the Russian revolution under Stalin.

My mind began to wander, and I was vaguely aware of Quentin using phrases such as "corruption of socialist ideals" and "dystopian allegory" as he explained the historic significance of each of the play's characters.

When he finally got round to my part, he said, "Now, Nancy. The Cat. You symbolize the *Lumpenproletariat*. Your feline charms belie your insincerity, in adhering to ideology for personal gain."

He smiled at me, and then moved on.

I'm sorry, my lumpen what? I thought.

I couldn't argue with the bit about insincerity and personal gain—as a cat that was second nature to me—but no one had ever described me as *lumpen* before, allegorically or otherwise. If anyone here could be described as lumpen it was the aging divorcée playing one of the shire horses. I began to wash furiously: I hadn't come here to be insulted.

But when I heard Quentin explain to a dozing Toffy that the Dog represented Stalin's secret police, I realized that his words needed to be taken with a pinch of salt. The idea that an overweight retriever could represent the ruthless enforcers of an authoritarian regime was laughable.

As the first rehearsal drew to a close Quentin waved his glasses around.

"Just one last thing, everybody; I've got one more cast member to introduce to you." He disappeared off the stage. A few moments later he returned, leading a confused-looking goat on a makeshift rope lead. The crowd "awwwed" in unison as Quentin said, "This is Fudge. She's going to be playing Muriel, the wise old goat, and, as those of you who have read your scripts will know, Muriel is one of the few animals on the farm who can read."

Well, that's just ridiculous, I thought, everyone knows goats can't read! Why on earth had this Orwell fellow written a book called *Animal Farm* when he clearly knew nothing about animals? I looked in Toffy's direction to see if he had noticed the irony, but he was fast asleep.

"Fudge will be joining us for the dress rehearsals and performances, when I also hope to have some other exciting additions to the cast as well."

I remained skeptical about Quentin's interpretation of the play's meaning and was also disappointed to see, upon flicking through the script, that the Cat did not actually have any lines to say. This seemed to me to be a gross underestimation of the role played by felines in historical events. I could see from the stage directions, however, that I would be onstage for most of the play's duration, and this went some way to soothing my bruised ego.

As rehearsals proceeded over the next few weeks I took the "Method" approach to my role, ingratiating myself with my fellow cast members purely for personal gain. I would curl up on their laps and allow them to stroke me, and in return they would offer me scraps from their sandwiches and saucers of milk. As the first night approached, excitement among the players began to grow. The performances would be taking place in the town's public hall, which could seat an audience of a couple hundred. I did my bit for publicity by circulating flyers to all the houses on my street and was gratified to hear my owners making reservations on the telephone for four seats on the opening night.

I tried to drum up interest among Team Nancy, too, but my friends were unanimous in their view that the public hall was too far from home for them to attend.

Finally opening night arrived. The cast gathered onstage for a technical run-through in full costume.

Fudge the goat had been tethered to a wooden post near the back of stage left. I was to sit on a stool next to Toffy at stage right.

The costume designer had made white masks for all the human's playing animal parts, which they wore with plain black clothes. It was not a naturalistic look, but I had to admit that, with the lighting rig in place, the overall effect was striking.

As we milled around, Quentin walked onto the stage.

"Quiet, everybody. I've got something to show you."

I turned to see him pushing a portable wooden chicken coop.

"In here are the finishing touches to our cast: the chickens, who, as you all know, represent the Russian peasantry. These bantams have very kindly been loaned to us for the performances. For obvious reasons," he said with a glance in my direction, "we won't be letting them out on stage."

He wheeled the coop over to where Fudge was standing, parking it alongside her post. The coop had wooden sides but its front consisted of a hinged chicken wire door.

As Quentin pushed it into place the hens and I made eye contact.

"Is that what I think it is?" I heard one of them cluck.

"Oh, my god. It's a cat. Where are we?" said another.

The human cast filed off the stage for one last cup of tea to settle their nerves. I was quite happy basking in the warmth of the stage lights so I stayed put, my calm mood disturbed only by the mutterings of the bantams.

After a while I heard the audience start to file into the hall on the other side of the curtain, their hushed voices murmuring as they flicked through their programs. Quentin led the rest of the cast back onto the stage and gave us a final pep talk as we took our positions for the first scene. I ran through my stage directions one last time in my mind: *Wash. Sit. Sleep. Look insincere.*

The audience fell silent as the lights dimmed in the hall, then the curtain rose and I looked out onto the darkened rows of faces. I could just about make out my owners and the little people, five rows back.

Act One was under way, and, true to the amateur dramatic tradition, the acting quality was patchy.

I could hear muffled clucking on the other side of the stage. Fudge the goat had got bored and begun to nuzzle the side of the coop, chewing at its edges and starting to paw at it with her front leg. Although I couldn't see them, I sensed that the hens were becoming agitated.

At the end of the third scene the lights dimmed, allowing for a quick reset of the stage. I hopped down from my stool and ran over to assume my next position beside a polystyrene tree.

The chicken coop was also repositioned for this scene, turned forty-five degrees to the left so that the chickens could now see the front section of the stage as well as the audience through their chicken wire door. This new position also meant that Fudge was within nuzzling distance of the hook-and-eye lock that held the door of the coop in place. I could tell she was fed up with being tethered to her post and was looking for new stimuli.

I can't speak for the audience, but I found myself becoming

more absorbed in the drama unfolding among the animals than in the one being acted out by the humans.

Act One was reaching its dramatic climax, in which the Pigs daubed the "Seven Commandments of Animalism" on the back wall of the stage. The cast chanted in unison:

"One. Two-legged beings are our enemies."

I watched as Fudge worked her way along the side of the coop, nibbling at the rough edges of the wood.

"Two. Four-legged beings are our allies and friends."

Her mouth reached the front corner of the coop, where the hook-and-eye fastening rattled precariously. Fudge seemed oblivious to everyone around her.

"Three. Animals shall never wear any clothes."

The bantams became increasingly agitated as they realized that some unseen animal was trying to get into their coop.

"Four. Animals shall never sleep in beds."

I looked at Toffy, who was following developments with an amused look on his face. He smiled and shrugged when I caught his eye. Fudge's nibbling mouth had now come into contact with the hook-and-eye lock, which shook for a few seconds before being dislodged by her tongue. The chicken wire door slowly swung open.

"Five. Animals shall never drink alcohol."

It took the hens a few seconds to realize that their coop was open, but once they did, they charged out en masse to the front of the stage.

Here they stopped, momentarily dazed, before squawking, "There's a cat! There's a dog! There are . . . people dressed as animals! What the hell is going on?!"

Then they dispersed in every direction in a frenzy of clucking.

The human cast gamely ignored the commotion, raising their voices to shouting-pitch in an attempt to drown out the noise of the hens.

"Six. Animals shall never kill animals."

Reader, I'm sure you know what's coming. I was no longer an

actor on a stage, a symbol of the lumpen proletariat. I was a ruthless killing machine, a destroyer of poultry. I was in Terminator mode, and as I looked around all I could see were flashing red targets indicating my prey.

Everywhere I looked there were panicking chickens, some attempting to fly into the backdrops, confused by the painted farmyard scenes. One charged straight forward to the edge of the stage and fell into the orchestra pit. I dropped to my haunches, stalking past Toffy, ignoring his protests of "Nancy, I'm not sure if that's such a good idea. . . ."

Then, as one of the hens that had attempted to fly into the scenery fell to the ground in a daze, I struck.

"Seven. All animals are equal."

The cast chanted around me, but I could no longer hear them. I dispatched my first victim easily—it was stunned by its collision with the backdrop and unable to put up much of a fight: one flick of the neck and it was dead. Seeing what I had done, the level of alarm among the other chickens increased tenfold.

"Oh, my god! Oh, my god!" they shrieked as they tried to seek shelter around the set.

One managed to flap up onto a branch of the polystyrene tree but soon discovered that it was not designed to take the weight of an amply proportioned avian. The tree creaked as it leaned to one side, gradually lowering the hen toward my expectant face.

It started flapping in an effort to evade my clutches, but I swung a paw out and grabbed the tip of one wing, snagging its feathers on my bared claws. Once I had the wing the rest was easy. I pulled the bird, still flapping, toward me, and plunged my teeth into its neck. The chicken was as big as me, and its free wing continued to flap, so I had no choice but to swing it around in a circle several times in order to break its neck. I noticed that, in its final, fear-filled moments, the hen's bowels opened, spraying the stage with excrement like water from a garden sprinkler.

Next I moved on to two hens who were hiding behind a bale of hay. They put up a good fight, and I had to use the "slasher" technique rather than the "neck snap," so the end result was rather messy. There were giblets, blood, and guts strewn all over the front of the stage, and I was vaguely aware of the town's mayor and other local dignitaries in the front row screaming and wiping themselves down.

I dispatched the fifth hen easily—she was frozen with fear behind the coop and didn't even attempt to fight.

Finally, I leapt into the orchestra pit, where I quickly cornered my last target and slaughtered it. Then, with its neck between my jaws and its innards trailing behind me, I jumped back onto the stage, instinctively dragging my prey back to my lair.

It was only at this point that I became aware that the performance had ground to a halt. I glanced up at the faces of my acting comrades. They were all staring at me in openmouthed horror. Their white animal masks were spattered with blood and excrement. Even Fudge had stopped nuzzling the coop and was regarding me with evident fascination.

I slowly turned to face the audience. There was complete silence in the hall. I could just about make out my owners in their seats, the grown-ups shielding the eyes of the little people, whose faces were contorted with fear. The only movement in the whole tableau was some feathers falling silently from the sky like confetti.

The next thing I knew, Quentin had rushed onto the stage, in what I thought was a very accurate impression of a panicked chicken. He stammered an apology and announced an early interval to allow for the stage to be cleaned and reset. Then he shrieked, "Curtain! Curtain!" and ran off.

It will probably not surprise you to hear that I did not hang around for Act Two.

As the curtain fell and the human cast began to sob, I darted into the wings, from where I was able to make a swift exit through the stage door.

I sat in the parking lot trying to gather my thoughts.

My stage debut hadn't exactly gone according to plan. But then, I was a cat, and what had Quentin expected me to do when faced with a half dozen lunatic birds running around in front of me?

He had wanted a memorable performance, an immersive audience experience, and I believed that was what he had got. It just wasn't memorable or immersive in quite the way he had intended.

Flicking some feathers from my paws, I considered the symbolic implications of my on-stage improvisations. In my version, the lumpen proletariat had slaughtered the peasantry. Okay, so that may not have been historically accurate, but surely, in a revolution, the peasantry were going to get slaughtered one way or another, right?

I heard the hall's front door open, and an audience member rushed out gasping for air, seemingly in the midst of a panic attack. I had planned to wait for my owners so I could get a lift home with them, but it occurred to me that I might now be *felis non grata*. And besides, after my killing extravaganza, I needed some fresh air.

I trotted along the side of the building, mentally crossing "Broadway star" off my list of career options.

As I cut across the shrubbery along the side of the parking lot I heard rustling to my left. I turned just in time to see a cat's tail disappear into the thicket.

"Who's that?" I whispered, but there was no reply.

Pondering this mystery as I made my way up the hill helped to take my mind off the telling-off that I knew would be waiting for me at home.

CHAPTER 16

MIAOW

*But fate ordains that dearest friends must
part.*

—Edward Young

A couple of days after my stage debut, or the Great Poultry Massacre, as my owners insisted on calling it, I poked my head around Murphy's kitchen door. He was sitting at the table clutching a glue stick between his paws.

"Oh, hi, Nancy! I'm just updating your cuttings album!" he said, cheerily waving a page from the local paper.

I had completely forgotten that the press had been in attendance, and my heart sank at the thought of what they might have written. Before I had a chance to stop him, Murphy started reading: "'Clucking hell! Nancy feline peckish on play's opening night.'"

I winced, but, figuring that I had probably heard the worst, I jumped up onto the table next to him.

Under the headline was a photo of me swinging a half-dead hen around my head as my human castmates looked on, aghast.

"Yep. That's pretty much how I remember it," I said.

"Wish I could have seen it . . . ," Murphy said wistfully as he pasted the page into the album.

"The press have had a field day," he continued. "'Feline thespian Nancy was accused of *fowl play* last night when she knocked *the stuffing* out of some chickens during a stage adaptation of *Animal Farm* . . . her *coop de grâce* only ended when all six chickens lay disemboweled on the stage. . . . She may prove to be the most infamous chicken killer since Colonel Sanders.'"

He laughed.

"So what's your next stage production going to be? *Chicken Run?*"

"Hmm. I think I might give the theater a miss for the time being," I replied. "Not sure it's really my thing after all."

"Shame," Murphy said, smoothing the page carefully into place with his paw.

We spent a pleasurable afternoon tormenting mice at the bottom of Murphy's garden until a fine drizzle set in and I decided to head home. Walking along the footpath I could not shake the feeling that I was being watched. Several times I stopped, convinced that I had seen movement out of the corner of my eye, but each time I looked there was no one there. I was walking up the grassy verge from the footpath toward my garden when I heard a rustle behind me.

I swung round to find myself face-to-face with a cat.

"Whoa!" I shouted involuntarily.

The cat, a haggard-looking black-and-white tom, smiled at me, motionless. He was wearing a pirate-style black patch over one of his eyes. As I looked quizzically at the patch he said, "Hi, Nancy. Remember me?"

He lifted a paw and slid the patch off, revealing a distinctive scar that ran from his forehead, across his eye, and down to his cheek.

"Number 29! Is that you?"

"Got it in one," he replied. "How've you been, Nancy?"

"I saw you on the news . . . your escape . . . but—how did you find me?" I stammered.

"Don't you remember? You told me about your life when you

were at the shelter. About NHQ and your people and Team Nancy. It all went in here," he said, tapping his head. He smiled uncertainly before adding, "I hope you don't mind."

"Of course I don't mind! How long have you been here?"

"Oh, a couple of months now. You could say I've been casing the joint. Loved your performance in *Animal Farm*, by the way," he said with a wink.

"That was *you*?" I shouted. "But why didn't you come to the house?"

Number 29 dropped his voice and whispered, "Couldn't do that, Nancy. I'm on the run, remember. If the police find me, they'll take me back to the shelter. Why do you think I've got this?" He held up the eye patch.

"I was wondering."

"It's a disguise. My face has been all over the news, hasn't it?"

"I suppose, but I'm not sure it's the best strategy if you want to blend in."

I thought for a few moments.

"Are you sure they'd take you back? If you like, I could ask my owners; I'm sure they'd be happy to—"

"Can't take that risk, Nancy. Besides, I've never had owners, have I? Too late to start now. There are plenty of sheds around for shelter, and I've been helping myself to food from the houses. Including yours. Street smarts, y'see," he said, tapping his head again.

"Well, in that case, come with me. I'll introduce you to the team."

He pulled his eye patch into place, and we set off through the garden.

"I'll take you to meet Brambles first," I said as we slipped under the trellis.

"Oh, yes, I've been having some fun with Brambles. Been moving his food bowl half an inch to the left when he's not looking. It's driving him mad!" He laughed.

"Yes, I imagine it is. Probably best not to tell him that."

"And who's that sour-faced calico on the other street? Doesn't like you much, does she?"

"That'll be Molly," I replied. "Just ignore her. It works for me."

I spent the afternoon introducing Number 29 to my friends, all of whom were in awe of his daredevil past. I hadn't planned to tell Pip about him, mainly because I thought Pip would disapprove of me for associating with a criminal. But the next morning he stumbled across us on the footpath, so I had no choice but to introduce them.

To my surprise Pip seemed to take an immediate liking to our new neighbor.

"Morning," he said, and Number 29 nodded in acknowledgment.

It occurred to me, on seeing them together for the first time, how similar looking they were (eye patch notwithstanding). They were both slim-built with long legs, and predominantly black-with-white socks and bibs.

They were so similar, in fact, they could almost have been brothers.

Perhaps the same thought occurred to them, as I thought I saw a flicker of recognition in their eyes, and although they didn't say much it seemed almost as if they shared an unspoken familiarity.

"Well, I'll leave you boys to it. I'd hate to intrude on the bromance," I joked, and they shot me identical dirty looks.

Number 29's appearance coincided with the arrival of summer. The days were warm and the garden was teeming with wildlife. For any other cat, life would have been sweet.

And yet, for me, there was something missing.

I logged on to Facebook one morning.

"What's on your mind?" prompted the status bar.

I wanted to type in, "What am I doing with my life? What happened to my career? Where am I going?"

I stared at the computer while the cursor flashed expectantly.

What *had* happened to my career? Since my foray into amateur dramatics, it was as if there was a consensus that the onstage killing spree had been my final fling with notoriety—my swan song—and that now I should keep out of the limelight.

I left the status bar blank and jumped down from the desk. I needed some fresh air to clear my head.

I walked to the top of the grassy verge behind the garden and sat looking down at the footpath. Then I heard a rustle in the undergrowth and Number 29 appeared by my side.

"All right, Nancy?" he asked. "Why so glum?"

"Oh, it's just . . . I really want to *do* something with my life. And I don't know what that is, but I know that I can't just hang around here forever, catching mice and going to the pub. I want a *career*. A *purpose*."

Number 29 looked slightly taken aback.

"Well, you did ask," I said.

"I want to be famous," I went on. "I want to be a celebrity. I want to be like . . . Madonna or Kate Winslet or . . . Lindsay Lohan."

At this a look of alarm flashed across Number 29's face.

"Well, maybe not *exactly* like Lindsay Lohan, but I want to make a name for myself, and I don't know how to go about it."

"Hmm. Tricky," he said thoughtfully. "What you really need is an agent."

I stared at him.

"Oh, my god!" I exclaimed. "Number 29, you're a genius!" I shouted, and I raced back to the house and upstairs to the study.

I was out of breath, so I took a few moments to settle myself on the desk, then typed, "cat + celebrity + agent," and clicked "search."

After scrolling through countless results offering agent details for Cat Deeley, I eventually came to a link for a website called A-List Felines. Under the agency's logo was a banner that read:

"I CAN MAKE YOUR CAT A STAR!"

Where do I sign? I thought. First I checked the contact details. There was no point getting an agent in America. Hollywood wasn't in my sights just yet. I was relieved to see a London phone number and address.

Next, what kind of work did this agent find? Since the online dating fiasco I knew I had to be on the lookout for weirdos.

The site gave examples of jobs the agent had found for her clients, including TV commercials, product tie-ins, and modeling for pet catalogs. It all sounded aboveboard.

Finally I checked out the agent herself. She was called Helen, and she looked to be in her midthirties, with shoulder-length brown hair and a warm smile. She described herself as a cat lover who had worked as a human celebrity agent for twelve years before deciding to specialize in felines. Prospective clients should e-mail a photo and résumé.

I selected a flattering photo and composed an e-mail in which I mentioned my singing and acting experience and attached a link to some of my press coverage. A short while later I received a reply from Helen, saying that she would read my cuttings and let me know within twenty-four hours whether she thought she could find work for me.

This is it, I figured. Amateur theater and local newspapers were one thing, but if I wanted to make it to the big time, I was going to need professional representation.

But what if she wrote back to say no, that she couldn't take me onto her books? What would I do then? It didn't bear thinking about.

I went into my owners' bedroom and curled up on the bed with my paws crossed under my chin. *Que sera sera*, I hummed. Whatever will be will be.

The following morning I pushed the study door shut behind me and turned the computer on.

Don't panic if she says no, I told myself, there are bound to be other agents out there. I scanned my in-box. In addition to the usual spam and Facebook notifications was an e-mail from Helen, with the subject heading "Work."

Hi, Nancy.

Thanks for your e-mail. I've read your press cuttings and I think I could take you on as a client. I should warn you that it can be difficult for black cats to find work (they don't photograph as well as lighter-colored cats), but I think with your personality and existing media profile we might be able to punch through in the marketplace.

The industry is London-based, so if you are serious about your career you will need to move to London. Several of my feline clients live at home with me, and I'd be willing to offer you the same arrangement.

If you are happy to proceed, I'll start preparing your contract.

Kind regards

Helen

Move to London. Everything else in the e-mail was a blur, but those three words leapt out at me. When I had thought about the possible answers Helen might give, this one hadn't even crossed my mind.

Of course the industry was based in London—I knew that, and it made sense to be near the heart of the action. But was I really prepared to give up my home and my friends for my career?

I closed the e-mail and began to wash.

When I had finished, I went to Murphy's house.

As Murphy's cat flap dropped shut behind me, I took a deep breath and sat down on his patio. He had taken my news pretty well, considering. I had feared another row like we'd had over my blog. I thought he would ask why a career was so important to me and why it wasn't possible to work but still live at home. But he hadn't.

He sat in silence while I explained that I needed to give my career one last shot, then he asked a few questions about the kind of work I would be doing. I explained that it would depend on the bookings Helen could get for me.

"I'm open-minded," I said. "I could be a model or an icon or an actress or whatever. A MIAOW, if you like!" We both laughed.

"How long will you stay at Helen's flat?"

"I'm not sure," I replied. "I guess we'll just see how it goes."

"I'll miss you," said Murphy.

"I know. I'll miss you, too. All of you."

At this he looked away, and when he turned back, his mouth was smiling but I could see the hurt in his eyes.

"Well, good luck! Knock 'em dead!" he said, trying to sound cheery.

"Will do," I replied, as grateful to him for what he hadn't said, as for what he had.

He walked me to the cat flap.

"You know I'll probably be back home in a week, with egg on my face, as usual."

"No, I don't think you will," he replied.

At home, I logged on to the computer, opened Helen's e-mail, and clicked "reply." Then I typed:

Hi, Helen,

That's all fine.

I'm on my way.

Nancy

CHAPTER 17

Living with the Competition

No cat is a hero to his agent.

—(Adapted from) Georg Hegel

I n the early hours of the morning I crept downstairs. My owners and Pip knew nothing of my plan to move to London, and I had decided to leave while they were still asleep, so as not to arouse their suspicion. The sun was rising over the park and the birds' dawn chorus was in full swing. I strode purposefully toward the train station, not stopping to contemplate the view. I did not want to think about when, or if, I would see this scene again.

It was the middle of the August vacation season, and at such an early hour the train station was empty. I was able to jump aboard the London-bound 6:15 and find my luggage crevice without anyone spotting me.

When I arrived at Helen's address, a house in north London that had been converted into flats, I launched myself, paws outstretched, at the intercom panel at the side of the front door. A few seconds later the door buzzed open, and I tiptoed up the dark stairwell of the house, for the first time feeling nervous about what lay ahead.

"Hello?" I mewed, tapping on the flat's front door with my paw. After a few moments a woman appeared in the doorway, having evidently just got out of bed. Her brown hair was a tangled mess and she wore a pair of faded, unironed pajamas. In addition to pillow crease marks on her cheek, her face bore the deeply etched lines of a habitual scowl. She did not look anything like the smiling lady on the website, and I deduced that the photo must be at least ten years out of date.

She frowned as she squinted at me through her haystack hair.

"Oh, you must be Nancy," she said distractedly. "You're early. Come in."

I walked into the flat, noticing a strong smell of stale cigarette smoke coming from her pajamas. I couldn't help but think of the last time I had been in this situation, when I first arrived at NHQ as a kitten. Here I was, almost exactly a year later, seeing another new home for the first time. But there were no excited little people here, and Helen did not seem inclined to make a fuss over me the way my owners had.

"I'll show you where everything is, and then you can meet the others," she said.

The door to her bedroom was closed. A sign hung from the handle, bearing a picture of a cat's face with a giant red cross through it and the words "Cat-Free Zone" underneath. I padded down the hallway after her. There was a small galley kitchen, a bathroom, and a living room, which also functioned as a home office. Helen opened another door.

"This is the cats' room."

I looked in and saw four beds on the floor, three containing sleeping cats and one empty, presumably intended for me.

"Everybody, this is Nancy. She's my new client."

Startled out of their sleep, the cats looked at me in varying states of confusion and disarray.

"Hi, everyone," I said shyly.

"That's Gerald, that's Oscar, and this is Princess," Helen said, pointing to them in turn. "The litter tray's here." She tapped the plastic box in the corner, which smelled like it needed changing. "Food and water by your bed. Right, I need a smoke and a cup of coffee." She closed the door and headed into the kitchen.

I looked around. Aside from the cat beds, the room was sparsely furnished. There was a tattered armchair by the window. Judging by the state of its upholstery its primary use was as a scratching post. Along one wall was a bookcase overflowing with piles of paperwork and empty cigarette packets. The beds were arranged so that each cat had its own corner of the room, and I could see that they had gone to some effort to personalize their space.

Gerald, a short-haired marmalade, had Blu-Tacked two posters to the wall. In one of the posters there were photos of him in a classic "before and after" layout.

In the "before" picture Gerald was hugely overweight, with rolls of fat bulging around his belly. His expression was miserable. In the "after" photo the smiling Gerald had slimmed down, proud of his newly svelte physique.

"I'm half the cat I used to be!" read the strapline across the bottom.

In the second poster the postdiet Gerald held up a huge cat collar, with a disbelieving look on his face.

"Look at the collar I used to wear!"

I smiled. Gerald had woken up now and was watching me intently.

"Pet Slimmer of the Year, you know," he said, by way of explanation.

"Congratulations!"

He gave me a complacent smile. "I'm the face of KittySlim cat food. This month alone I've done daytime television and been featured in *Take a Break* magazine."

"Wow," I said, impressed.

I looked at the food bowl next to Gerald's bed. The dry food pellets in there looked like they were made of cardboard.

"Does it taste nice?" I asked.

"Try it for yourself," he replied.

I picked a pellet out of his bowl. Sure enough, it tasted of cardboard. He looked at me expectantly.

"Mmm. It's probably an acquired taste, isn't it?" I said, trying to be diplomatic. "I think I'm more of a Kit-e-Licious girl, really."

Gerald shrugged.

I was distracted by a mechanical whirring noise and looked over at Oscar, a black long-haired tom. He had his paw on the button of an automated card-shuffling device, which he pressed in short bursts. Oscar had no posters, but there was a pile of books on the floor next to his bed with titles like *You, Too, Can See the Future* and *Mind Reading for Beginners*.

I smiled at Oscar, fairly confident that I knew his line of work.

"Let me guess. Are you . . . a magician?"

Oscar's jaw dropped, and he inadvertently held his paw down on the button of the shuffling machine, sending cards flying in every direction.

"I. Am not. A magician. I am. A psychic." He spoke slowly, enunciating each word with care.

"Oh, right, I see," I replied, still confused.

"Have you not read about me in the papers? I predicted the results of every match in the World Cup finals this summer. You must have seen the headlines."

"No, I don't think I did. That's very impressive, though. So what's next, now the World Cup's over?"

A slight frown appeared on Oscar's brow.

"You're as bad as Helen!" he muttered. "I'm working on a new card act. All will be revealed in due course."

He began to gather up the spilled cards and insert them back into the machine.

Princess's bed was next to the bookcase on the other side of the room. She was a lilac Persian, with long, perfectly groomed fur and a round, squashy face. She had placed a pink silk screen alongside her bed to demarcate her boudoir area. She had also appropriated the bottom shelf of the bookcase, where she kept a pedestal mirror, an assortment of combs, and a selection of collars and eye masks.

"Model?" I asked.

"That's right," Princess said, a hint of Persian snuffle in her voice. "Glamour puss, actually. Calendars, high-end fashion stuff. No catalog work," she added quickly.

"Wow. I entered a cat show once," I said, thinking of the Persians I had encountered in Birmingham. "Do you ever do shows?"

Princess harrumphed disdainfully. "Never! Those places are like meat markets. Yuck!"

"Yes, I know what you mean," I replied, relieved that we at least had one thing in common.

"So, what do *you* do?" Oscar asked.

"Um, well, I'm not quite sure yet. I've done a bit of acting—theater stuff mostly—and singing. . . ." I trailed off, aware of how flimsy my answer sounded.

It struck me for the first time that I was in the company of professionals. These cats were not like Team Nancy, amazed that a cat could do anything other than eat, sleep, and hunt. They knew what their talent was, and they worked hard at exploiting and publicizing it.

The cats looked at me, waiting for me to continue.

"I thought I might become a MIAOW: a model, icon, actress . . . or . . . whatever. . . ." I trailed off again, seeing that they were all staring at me blankly. The acronym that had made Murphy laugh did not cut any ice with these three.

"An icon? How can a cat be an icon?" Oscar asked, his eyes narrowing.

"Oh, it's just a joke really. I needed a word beginning with 'I' or it wouldn't have made sense. It would have been MAOW. . . ." I trailed off for a third time, making a mental note not to mention my acronym to anyone in the business, ever again. At least not unless I could come up with a better word beginning with "I."

"So how long have you all lived here?" I asked, desperate to change the subject.

"I've been here a year," said Gerald.

"Six months," said Princess.

"Helen signed me up in June," Oscar added.

"What's it like? Is Helen nice?"

The cats looked nonplussed.

"She's okay." Gerald shrugged.

"She does her job and we do ours. It's business," explained Oscar.

"Oh."

Of course it was business. I was going to have to get used to this new, professional mindset.

I suddenly felt overcome by tiredness and walked over to the empty bed. "Think I might just take a nap," I said, aware that the other cats were still scrutinizing me.

As I stepped in, I wondered how many other cats had occupied this bed before me, and what had happened to them and their careers.

The threadbare tartan fabric reminded me of the bed at the shelter, which in turn made me think of Number 29. Then an image of him and Pip side by side on the footpath popped into my mind, quickly followed by an image of my people at NHQ. I wondered whether they had noticed I was missing, and if so, whether they assumed I was at the park or the pub, bound to reappear later in the day.

I curled up into a neat ball, happy to think of home as I let sleep take me.

I was woken by a strange noise, and my first thought was that I was back at the shelter, listening to Number 29 scratching at the wall. As I came round I realized that Oscar's card shuffler was whirring into action. I stood up, still sleepy, and noticed that

Princess and Gerald were no longer in the room and the door was open. Oscar seemed absorbed in his cards, so I hopped out of my bed and walked into the hallway.

I stood at the doorway to the living room. Helen was sitting at the desk with her back to me. She was typing on her laptop, cigarette in hand, while talking on the phone. Or, to be exact, shouting on the phone.

"No, I'm sorry, that's *not* acceptable," she fumed, blowing smoke out through the side of her mouth. "That's not what I said and that isn't what we agreed. . . . No, I didn't . . ." (suck on cigarette). "Look, if you're going to talk to me like that I'm going to have to put the phone down . . ." (exhale of smoke).

I hovered in the doorway, not wanting to draw Helen's attention lest I become the next object of her wrath. After a few more minutes of arguing Helen said, "Fine," before slamming the phone down and giving a strangled screech.

"For God's sake, why are there so many *idiots* in this business?" she shouted, lighting up another cigarette.

Gerald walked past on his way to the bathroom, rolling his eyes.

"Is she always like that?" I whispered.

"Pretty much," he replied.

Helen sat at the desk, muttering. Suddenly the sound of a cat hissing and spitting behind me made me jump. I spun round, but there were no cats in sight, just Helen's handbag on the floor by the front door. I felt my hackles rising. The noise started again, and this time I could tell it was coming from inside Helen's bag. Could she have another cat in there?

Before I had a chance to investigate, Helen swore, then got up from her seat and stomped toward the door. There was no time for me to dash into another room, so I pressed myself against the wall, praying that she wouldn't notice me or, even worse, think that I was responsible for the noise. As she stormed past me toward her bag the hissing noise started again.

"All right! I'm coming, for God's sake!"

She delved into the bag and rummaged around before pulling out her mobile phone, which was emitting what I now realized was an angry-cat ringtone. She held the phone to her ear.

"Hello? Yes, I *am* busy. What do you want?" she snapped at the caller before stomping back into the living room.

She had not even noticed me.

I sat in the hallway, my nerves jangling. I would have to develop a thicker skin if I was to flourish in this new environment. My eyes rested on the bathroom door, which was ajar.

Hang on a minute, I thought. Didn't Gerald just go in there?

I crept up and poked my head around the door, to see Gerald squatting on the toilet seat.

"Gerald, what *are* you doing?" I asked.

"What do you think I'm doing?" he replied. He turned around to press the flush and jumped down.

"What on earth is that?" I said, looking at the ring-shaped object resting on the toilet seat.

"It's a Litter Kwitter. Haven't you ever seen one before?"

"No."

I was intrigued. I walked over to examine the device more closely.

Brambles would love one of these, I thought. Then I sighed. These professional cats were so much more worldly than I was.

Helen had gone into the kitchen to make another cup of coffee, so I padded into the living room. On the coffee table was a pile of cuttings albums, one for each cat client. As I looked at them I tried not to think about the album Murphy had lovingly put together for me at home.

Oscar's was on the top of the pile. On the first page was a cutting from a tabloid newspaper.

"A-meow-zing! Mystic mog sees football's future!" was the headline.

Underneath was a photo of Oscar, a solemn expression on his face, pointing to a bowl of food labeled with the Spanish flag. The fawning article reported how "fur-tune-telling feline Oscar

INCREDIBLY predicted the result of the World Cup finals. The psychic kitty chose food from bowls marked with the flags of the competing nations. Every time, Oscar has chosen food from the bowl of the winning side, and now bookmakers are racing to offer the prophet puss a job."

I smiled as I read the article. Did anyone really believe this stuff? It was a fifty-fifty chance each time; a string of lucky guesses: there was nothing more to it than that. He'd better hope his new card trick is good, I thought, or Oscar's career will be over before the summer's out.

Gerald's album was full of advertisements for KittySlim.

One read, "Tubby Tabby? Try the KittySlim challenge! You could lose two collar sizes in four weeks!"

I couldn't help but laugh at Gerald's expression in the photos. I could imagine the photographer instructing him, "Look miserable! You're fat! No one likes you!" at the "before" photo shoot, then, "Smile! You're gorgeous!" for the "after" shot.

The album also contained the "true story" feature from *Take a Break* magazine, showing a snapshot of fat Gerald fast asleep, his flesh spilling out from his body in folds.

On the facing page was a full-length portrait of the sleek postdiet Gerald.

"I used to get the cream—but look at me now!" the article was titled, and it told the "incredible" story of how Gerald had "clawed his way back to shape" by undertaking the KittySlim diet plan. The article ended with a quote from Gerald: "If I can do it, so can you!"

I must send a copy of this to Molly, I thought.

Princess's album contained page after page of glamour photos, in which she tilted her head to one side and pouted at the camera, the same vacant look in every shot. There was very little to read in her album, apart from one profile piece detailing her "vital cat-istics" and giving the secrets of her beauty regime. Princess was a cat who traded on looks alone, I realized.

A fourth book lay, as yet untouched, on the coffee table. Presumably this was going to be my album. I flicked through it and wondered what cuttings were destined to cover its empty pages. My stomach fluttered with trepidation and excitement. Helen's flat was not exactly a home away from home, but I had come this far and I had no choice but to keep going. My career lay in front of me, literally a blank page. How to fill it was up to me.

CHAPTER 18

Screen Queen

Dreaming about being an actress is more
exciting than being one.

—Marilyn Monroe

R ight, Nancy, I've had a job come through that might suit
you."

It was about a week after my arrival and I was dozing in bed,
but my ears pricked up at the word "job."

I followed Helen into the living room, where she sat down at
her laptop and began to read from an e-mail.

"It's for a TV commercial," she said. "Cat charity. Fund-
raising ad. You know the kind of thing."

I didn't, but I nodded anyway, not wanting to look like an
amateur.

"They want plain-looking alley-cat types, nothing fancy.
You'll be perfect."

I bit my lip. I knew that, as a black cat, I was going to have to
get used to such prejudice. And besides, I figured *any* TV commercial must be a good way to start an acting career.

Helen scrolled through the e-mail with one hand on the
mouse, while the other hand rummaged across her desk seeking
out her cigarettes and lighter. She grabbed a cigarette, shoved it
between her lips, and lit it without taking her eyes off the screen.

"Shoot's tomorrow at eight a.m. We'll set off from here at seven."

And with that she took a long suck on the cigarette, slammed the laptop shut, and stood up. This, I realized, was my cue to leave.

I walked back into the bedroom, wondering whether I was, finally, on the cusp of a career breakthrough.

I looked at Princess, who was combing her long fur in front of the mirror.

"I've got my first job tomorrow, Princess. A TV commercial!"

"Good for you," she replied distractedly, tugging at a tangle behind her ear.

"It's for a cat charity. Have you ever done one of those?"

Princess shot me a look.

"I'm a glamour puss! I'm far too attractive to be in a charity commercial!"

She turned back to her mirror and resumed her battle with the tangle, evidently unaware of the insult implicit in her words.

The following morning I awoke to the sound of Helen crashing around in the bathroom. I heard Gerald's Litter Kwitter seat being knocked off the toilet and clattering noisily onto the floor tiles.

"F***ing thing!" Helen yelled as she kicked it across the room.

I had become used to being woken in this manner, but as I yawned, it struck me that today was officially the start of my new career: I was a working actress.

All my roommates were still asleep, so I crept over to peer in Princess's mirror. My reflection looked back at me sleepily. I practiced a few smiles like I had seen Princess do many times.

Who are they calling plain-looking? I said to myself.

Then I had a few mouthfuls of food from my bowl, eased

open the bedroom door, and went into the hallway to wait for Helen, who was now slamming drawers in the kitchen and, judging by the smell, burning a piece of toast. At quarter to eight she ran into the hallway and shouted, "We're *late*! Where are my bloody shoes?"

I pointed to the heap of jumbled-up shoes inside the front door, and she pounced upon them, throwing random mismatched trainers and boots over her shoulder until she located a pair of pumps.

"Right, come on, then," she muttered, holding the door open for me. I slipped through the doorway and down the stairs.

Outside, Helen opened the trunk of her sporty compact and I realized I would not be riding alongside her in the passenger seat. Clearly, the leather upholstery was, like Helen's bedroom, a "cat-free zone."

I compliantly jumped into the trunk, and once she had slammed the door shut, I made myself a makeshift bed among the coats. After a half-hour drive, the car stopped and I could hear Helen's footsteps on tarmac. Even her footsteps sounded angry, I noticed. She swung the door open.

"We're here. Come on, get out."

We had parked next to a huge windowless building that looked, from the outside, like an aircraft hangar. There were lots of people rushing around, carrying metal boxes into the building from vans parked outside.

A portable office stood in the parking lot, with a makeshift sign on the window saying "Feline Rescue: Production Office." I sat on the hood of Helen's car while she went inside.

A car drove past and parked in the disabled spot right outside the hangar. A woman stepped out of the car, carrying a cat basket. She placed the basket on the ground, then she disappeared into the office, too.

Eventually Helen reemerged with an ID tag around her neck.

"Come on, Nancy. You're going in there." She pointed to the hangar's entrance.

The building's interior had been sectioned off with plywood screens, and in one of the sections a cluster of people were setting up lights and maneuvering cameras into place. I slalomed between people's legs and around the power cables that trailed across the floor, keen to get a better view. I could hear meows coming from behind the screens.

Dodging a huge light on a tripod I finally saw the set: an eerily accurate re-creation of the inside of a cat shelter, just like the one I had spent a night in after New Year. There was a long row of hutches, each having its temporary cat resident installed. I couldn't help but think of Number 29 and wonder what he would make of this show business version of his old life. A man with a clipboard and a baseball cap swung round as I approached, checking his list.

"You must be Nancy."

I nodded and Helen said, "Correct."

"Great. You're playing Feral Cat Number 5. In there, please." And he pointed to one of the hutches.

Feral Cat Number 5? The casting specification for "plain-looking" cats made sense now. I had not been cast in this commercial for my talent or my personality, but because I looked like the kind of cat who could be feral. The kind of cat whom nobody in their right mind would want as a pet.

I made my way toward hutch number 5, wondering if the Kit-e-Licious cat ever had to endure this kind of blatant miscasting.

I jumped into the hutch and immediately spotted the art department's first inaccuracy: the tartan bed was brand-new, its quilted lining still firm and plump. There had been nothing firm and plump about the bed I had slept in at the real shelter. The hutch walls also smelled of fresh paint, and although they had the appearance of solid brick they wobbled when I touched them. After a few minutes the paint fumes made me light-headed, so I settled down to observe the scene beyond my hutch door.

I recognized the woman who had parked in the disabled spot

outside. She carefully lifted her feline charge out of his cat box and placed him in the hutch next to mine. He was a gray-and-white tabby with one front paw tightly wrapped in a bandage. As his handler held him he glanced at me with a pained expression.

All around me the hutches were filling up and I could hear some of the cats greeting each other, obviously seasoned pros. They chatted sagely about the state of the industry and moaned about how slow things always got over the summer. A couple of cats were sharing a hutch, and as we waited for the shoot to get going, they practiced their facial expressions and discussed their motivation. Then they sat in silence for a few moments, before halfheartedly nibbling the cat biscuits in their bowl and complaining about the quality of the catering.

Eventually one of the crew members in jeans and T-shirt came and stood in front of the hutches.

"Can I have everyone's attention, please," he shouted.

The murmuring died down.

"We're ready to roll for take one, the establishing shot of all our poor, homeless cats. Can all the talent please try and look miserable."

I looked around, wondering who "the talent" were, but quickly gathered from the way the other cats had reacted that it was us. I closed my eyes and tried to summon up my state of mind when I had been at the real shelter, wondering whether my owners would ever find me.

The camera slowly rolled along on tracks in front of us, each cat doing its best to convey misery into the lens.

"Very good, everybody. Now, in our next scene someone is coming to choose a cat to take home. I need you all to look expectant and hopeful."

We duly obliged, looking alert and pricking up our ears, but the director was dissatisfied.

"Come on, I need to see some movement, show a bit more enthusiasm! You need to get noticed if you want to be re-homed!"

I launched myself at the wire door, scrabbling as high as I could and clinging on while yowling like a crazed banshee.

"That's more like it!" the director shouted encouragingly, and all around me cats were meowing, writhing on the floor, or pawing at their hutch doors.

When the actress saw me hanging off my door for dear life she looked faintly alarmed and quickly moved on to the next hutch, where the cat with the bandaged paw was lying.

She'll never be interested in him, I thought, but to my great surprise the director called, "Cut!" and then told the actress to look tearful as she contemplated the injured kitty.

Still hanging from the door, I realized I could no longer feel my toes, so I unhooked my claws and tumbled, rather inelegantly, to the floor. I then sat and watched in disbelief as the actress was won over by the invalid cat's fragile vulnerability and decided to take him home.

The sequence needed to be filmed several times to get the requisite shots from different angles, and I could tell the director and the rest of the production team were getting tired and frustrated, rather like the little people at NHQ when they were over-hungry. Instead of the relaxed smiles and friendly banter, there were now furrowed brows and snappy exchanges.

In the absence of any further instructions from the director, I returned to my bed and resumed my default "miserable" pose, before drifting into a light snooze.

Eventually the director said, "Well done, everybody. We'll break for lunch and should have a rough cut to show you all before you leave."

I had no idea what a rough cut was but I knew what lunch was, and I instantly ran to the front of my hutch, waiting for someone to come and unlock the door. A catering van was parked just outside the set, so I and the rest of the talent filed outside and formed a queue.

One Kit-e-Licious pouch later, I felt my normal self again.

Most of the cats were milling around in front of the catering van, chatting about the commercial and hoping for scraps of food from the production team. One cat had jumped into the plastic garbage can, in search of leftovers, and managed to topple the whole thing to the ground, whereupon he dashed out, looking embarrassed. The other cats gave him disapproving looks and made a few barbed comments about his lack of professionalism.

Eventually the director reappeared and announced that the rough cut was ready to view and we should all gather inside. I and the other cats made our way back onto the set and assembled in front of a small monitor perched on top of a metal box. The director stood close by, ready to read out the voice-over, which would be added in the postproduction phase. The room hushed, and the director pressed play.

The commercial started with a slow-motion shot as the camera slid past the row of hutches, each cat emanating misery.

The director intoned in a somber voice: "Nobody wanted these cats. They were all abandoned and unloved. Discarded family pets, rejected because they weren't cute enough."

The director spoke the words "weren't cute enough" just as the camera lingered outside my hutch. I raised my eyebrows and looked around to see if anyone else had noticed the incongruity of words and pictures, but they were all staring intently at the screen.

"Some of these cats were abandoned as kittens and have antisocial behavioral problems, which have made them difficult to re-home."

Now the screen showed me hanging by my claws from the door of my hutch with a demonic look on my face, before tumbling to the floor.

"Hang on a minute, that's not fair, you told us to liven things up a bit!" I protested, but no one was listening. One cat at the back of the group said, "Shh!" so I had no choice but to turn back to the monitor.

Now the cat with the bandaged paw was on-screen.

"This is Hansel. Hansel was hit by a car and survived in the wild for three weeks before being brought to the shelter. Here he received life-saving medical assistance. He was lucky not to lose his paw."

The director sounded like he was on the verge of tears, as Hansel's face looked pleadingly into the camera.

Then, with a new note of optimism in his voice, he continued: "But here at Feline Rescue, we believe all our cats deserve a chance at happiness. Even injured ones like Hansel."

I winced. Who had written this dreadful, sentimental script? I could have done a better job.

On-screen, the actress opened the door of Hansel's hutch and lifted him out to cuddle him over her shoulder. The camera zoomed in on Hansel's face, which was now beaming with satisfaction.

"Please give whatever you can afford to help Feline Rescue save more cats like Hansel."

The image froze on Hansel's smug face.

There was a moment's silence before a ripple of self-congratulatory applause spread across the production team and the cats murmured their approval. I looked around to see Hansel with tears in his eyes, being congratulated on his performance. My tail began to twitch as I ruminated on my portrayal in the commercial. "Not cute enough," "antisocial," and "behavioral problems" were the phrases that had variously been used to describe me. Not exactly flattering.

The production team began to disperse, and the cats' handlers reappeared with boxes. As I waited for Helen, who was outside smoking a cigarette, I saw Hansel's agent walk over to him. I watched in disbelief as she carefully unwrapped the bandage from his paw. Hansel sighed with relief and flexed his leg a few times before trotting off happily toward the exit.

Bloody hell, I thought. (Helen's constant swearing had started to rub off on me.) He's not even disabled!

I began to wash, wondering if anything one saw on TV was actually true.

Eventually, after all the other cats had been collected, Helen rushed onto the set, a scowl on her face, saying, "There you are. Come on, we've got to go."

Back at the flat, Gerald was balancing on a set of scales next to his bed.

"How'd it go?" he asked when I walked in, lifting one paw off the scales to see if it made any difference to the flickering digital display.

"Okay, I think, if you can call being described as 'not cute enough' and 'antisocial' okay."

"You're a black cat, aren't you? Par for the course. You'll have to get used to it," he replied, stepping off the scales. "A job's a job, though, so don't knock it."

I knew he was right, but I wondered if I was wasting my time trying to build an acting career. I knew the dangers of typecasting and that I would only ever be cast in the "plain-looking" roles.

I stepped into my bed and started to lick my front paws. I had imagined acting would be exciting and glamorous, but in fact it was anything but. Instead of fruit baskets and limos there had been a wobbly set that smelled of paint, and the pitch-black trunk of Helen's car. And as if that weren't bad enough, my character had been grossly misrepresented in the end product.

I mentally crossed out the "A" in MIAOW. Acting, on reflection, probably wasn't for me. But that still left model, icon, or whatever.

Tomorrow, I decided, I would start at the beginning, with "M."

CHAPTER 19

Model Nancy

*Great art picks up where the call of nature
ends.*

—(Adapted from) Marc Chagall

The following day, Helen left the flat early for a meeting, so I took advantage of the peace and quiet to log on to her laptop. I opened Google and typed "cat model" in the search bar. Topping the results was a rather disreputable-looking agency seeking "adult cats for adult pictures."

One for the Online Vice Squad, I chuckled.

There was also a feline modeling agency, although the small print revealed that an "administration fee" had to be paid up front, and that the agency could not guarantee that it would find work for its clients.

A mug's game, I decided, inwardly pleased with my growing industry savvy.

Just as I was about to give up and try to think of a different profession beginning with "M," I stumbled across the website of a cat who had started his career as an artist's model, but subsequently made a name for himself as a painter.

I was intrigued. Artist's model had not even crossed my mind as a profession, but it did have a certain bohemian air to it.

The website featured a photo of an overweight orange tom sprawled on an artist's easel, wearing an expression of indifferent superiority. Displayed on the easel was a canvas covered in smears of paint, in which the traces of paw prints could just be made out. To me, the painting looked like a canvas that had been walked across by a cat with dirty paws, but upon closer examination it emerged that there had been an exhibition of these "paw-print paintings" in a gallery in east London.

The cat's owner, an artist himself, had coauthored a series of paintings entitled *Cat: Reinvented*, in which the cat had, "using his paws as tools, had through the medium of gouache, expressed the fundamental angst of the feline condition."

It sounded ludicrous to me, but when I read that the entire collection had been snapped up by Charles Saatchi, I decided I should keep an open mind regarding artistic merit. Who was I to argue with the informed opinion of the art establishment?

The cat went by the name of 🐾, believing that a conventional name functioned as a label, which in turn would stifle his creativity. Pretentious, undoubtedly, but I was beginning to realize that this went with the territory where art was concerned.

I dropped 🐾 an e-mail at theartistformerlyknownasfluffy@catpainter.com, expressing my admiration for his work and wondering if he might need a model for his next project.

As I finished the e-mail, Princess walked into the living room and hopped up onto the sofa.

"Princess, have you ever been an artist's model?" I asked her.

"A what?" she said, looking at me blankly.

"A model for an artist. You know, having your portrait painted."

She ruminated for a few moments, mulling the concept over in her mind.

"No, I haven't," she said. "I don't think my target demographic is into fine art. Photos, calendars, glamour, yes. Paintings, no. First rule of modeling, Nancy: know your audience."

I was taken aback by the astuteness of her reply. Maybe there was more to being a glamour puss than I had given Princess credit for.

I jumped down from the desk and went into the bedroom to get something to eat. I picked a few morsels of dry food from my bowl, keeping one eye on Oscar. He was on the other side of the room lining up various objects next to his bed: a toy mouse, a tennis ball, a roll of Scotch tape. He was staring at them all intently, taking meticulous care over the positioning of each object.

"Oscar, have you got OCD?" I asked, swallowing my last mouthful.

"No, of course I haven't," he replied with a scowl. "I'm practicing."

"For your next trick?" I said.

He stopped what he was doing and looked at me.

"How many times do I have to tell you, I do not do *tricks*. I am a psychic, not a magician."

I was dying to ask him why he needed to practice, if he was psychic, but instead I said, "Well, I can't wait to see the result."

"All in good time," he murmured.

I went back into the living room and jumped up onto the desk. I was thrilled to see a reply from 🐾 in my in-box. It was a brief message, in which he said that he was taking a break from painting at the moment, but that his owner was working on his next cat-themed collection and would be interested in finding a new feline creative partner. He suggested I come to the studio to meet them both.

"Wow, that's lucky!" I said out loud, although I could hear from her snuffly snores that Princess was asleep on the sofa.

I left the e-mail open on the laptop and curled up opposite Princess on the sofa to wait for Helen's return.

At about three o'clock I heard Helen's key in the lock, shortly followed by her voice. She was talking on her mobile phone, and she sounded cross.

I sighed, wondering if she had any emotional setting other than angry.

She dropped her handbag inside the front door and kicked off her shoes, then went into the kitchen and put the kettle on. I tried to suppress the nervous flutterings in my stomach. Would Helen be annoyed that I had found myself a job?

She carried her cup of coffee into the living room and sat down at the desk. She lit a cigarette, inhaled deeply, then turned to her laptop. I held my breath as she looked at the screen, evidently reading my e-mail.

She looked at me and said sharply, "Nancy, is this yours?" and I smiled and nodded.

"Artist's model," she said, then paused. "Good idea. Could be a lot of money in that, if we can copyright your image. I'll send this guy an e-mail and sort something out."

Was that it? I couldn't believe that Helen had accepted my suggestion so willingly. Surely the omens were looking good for the letter "M."

The following morning, I climbed into Helen's trunk and we set off for east London. The studio was in a converted warehouse in Hoxton, which from the outside looked unfit for human habitation, but of course the shabby exterior was misleading, and the interior had been fully renovated while maintaining an air of industrial functionality. Helen and I took the trade-style elevator to the top floor and walked out into an open-plan studio-cum-living-space.

🐾's owner, the artist, was the first to meet us.

He was a somewhat oddly dressed young man, with what looked like four different haircuts on his head and an apparently random selection of clothes on his body, all of which seemed either too small or too large for him. Helen stepped forward to shake his hand, and they began to discuss the terms of our arrangement.

While they talked, I walked across the studio to a huge floor-to-ceiling window through which sunlight was falling in great shafts. In one of the shafts of light, spread-eagled on a drawing board, was 🐾.

"You must be Nancy," he murmured, hardly moving a muscle as he looked me up and down. I nodded and opened my mouth to return the greeting, before realizing that I wasn't entirely sure what name I should use.

"I really love your work," I stammered.

I surveyed the various canvases stacked around the room, but in all honesty was unable to tell which had been painted by the cat and which by the owner. I looked over at Helen, who was full of smiles and charm toward the artist. He was blushing slightly and laughing at her jokes. In that moment, I found a new respect for Helen's professional abilities.

Helen and the artist started to walk toward us and I noticed as they did so that the artist's shoes did not match.

"Let's have a look at you, then," he said to me, placing his hand under my chin and turning my face from side to side.

"Okay, she'll be fine," he said to Helen. "She'll need to move into the studio for a couple of weeks while I work."

"Perfect," Helen said. "I'll get those contracts in the post."

From now on, it seemed, I was to be an artist's model.

Once she had gone, the artist walked over to another part of the studio to prepare his materials, or possibly to look at himself in the mirror and rectify the mistakes he had made while getting dressed.

I was now alone with 🐾, who was flat on his back on the drawing board, his eyes shut and his paws lolling over the edges. He appeared to have forgotten that I was there.

"So what does being an artist's model involve, exactly?" I asked.

"Oh, don't worry, you won't be doing any of the creative work yourself. Leave that to the experts. All you have to do is be yourself, sit still, and try not to get in the way."

Realizing that I would not be expected to wade through paint was a great relief.

I pictured myself immortalized on canvas, like one of Stubbs's horses or Velázquez's dogs.

Over the next two weeks, I spent many hours "being myself" in the name of art. The first time I modeled I was nervous, of course. The artist had placed a velvet cushion on a plinth next to a small storage heater, and as I had a final wash behind a bamboo screen I felt a few butterflies in my stomach. But like a true pro, I slipped my collar off and emerged from behind the screen without a backward glance. I assumed my position on top of the plinth, where the warmth from the heater quickly made me fall asleep.

In the breaks between modeling I explored the studio, and I discovered there were some perks to a bohemian lifestyle. There was certainly a lot less shrieking in the studio than in Helen's flat, and fewer rules regarding where I was allowed to sleep. There were also numerous canvases stacked against each other, which I could explore, and random objects including bicycle wheels hanging from the walls to provide me with exercise. Like Helen's flat, there was no access to outside space, but I was impressed by the toilet facilities—a sleek chrome litter tray, designed by Philippe Starck.

An old-fashioned iron birdcage dangled tantalizingly from the ceiling in one part of the room, and I spent many hours launching myself at it from different angles, desperate to see what was inside. 🐾 observed my efforts with his usual enigmatic smile (which, to be honest, was beginning to grate on me). I finally managed to springboard from the back of a rocking chair and catch hold of the filigree detailing on the side, where I held my position just long enough to see that there was nothing inside except a solitary egg glued to the perch. I lost my footing and dropped to the floor, to the sound of a derisive snort from 🐾.

"You could have told me there were no birds in there!" I protested, but he merely raised an eyebrow at me.

"It's art, darling; of course there are no birds in there."

"Doesn't look much like art to me," I muttered.

"Surrealism, dearie. Haven't you ever heard the term?"

I wanted to say, "Haven't you ever heard the term 'pretentious windbag'?" but I held my tongue.

A routine emerged whereby I would spend the days napping on my plinth cushion, eating, washing, and napping again while the artist busied himself in the studio and 🐾 slept on the drawing board. I chose not to look too closely at the work in progress, preferring to save the "big reveal" for the opening night of the exhibition.

A couple of days before the launch a delivery of catalogs arrived. The artist ripped open the box excitedly and began to read out the explanatory notes for *Cat: Deconstructed*.

"'An exploration of the human in juxtaposition to the feline, of our shared mortality and visceral natures,'" he read aloud.

It sounded like gobbledygook to me, but the artist was pleased, and I couldn't wait to see the paintings on display.

The day of the opening was marked with excitement for me, an apparently blasé indifference for 🐾, and a complete nervous breakdown for the artist. The gallery sent several vans to transport the "pieces" (as I had learned to refer to them), and once these had all been dispatched, the three of us set off for the gallery in the artist's car.

"Not a bad turnout," he muttered as we approached the gallery's entrance.

The sound of clinking glasses and a hubbub of voices was coming from inside. As we walked into the lobby the assembled crowd greeted us with an impromptu round of applause. I was not surprised to see various people dressed in the same manner as the artist, that is to say, in clothes seemingly selected at random from the contents of a recycling bin. I deduced they were probably artists, too.

I helped myself to some canapés that were being handed round by waitresses in the lobby, before proceeding through a door into the exhibition room.

My first inkling that the exhibition might not be what I had anticipated came as I walked through the doorway.

I know that smell, I thought. That smells like . . . litter tray!

Refusing to believe my nose I followed the crowd into a large, square room, which was painted white from floor to ceiling. Sure enough, the first sight that greeted me was the contents of the Philippe Starck litter tray I had been using for the previous fortnight, laid out on the floor in mounds of varying size and consistency. Stunned, I read the explanatory card placed alongside the display:

"An exploration of the human impulse of revulsion toward our own animalistic functions."

As if that made things any clearer!

I looked up to see how the humans were reacting to this assault on their senses, and although a few of them were pretending not to have noticed the stench of feces and ammonia, and were looking with rapt concentration at the "art," I also saw that several of them had instinctively recoiled, to busy themselves with their catalogs and champagne.

Working my way around the exhibition I encountered humiliation heaped upon humiliation. Beyond the—excuse my language but I believe in calling a spade a spade—piles of cat shit, I discovered a Perspex cube containing clumps of my fur, and a row of petri dishes in which my nail clippings had been suspended in formaldehyde.

On a plinth in the middle of the gallery were the remains of a mouse I had caught at the studio. It had been reassembled, but with its limbs and head reattached in the wrong places, so that its face was poking out of its armpit, and instead of a face it had a tail. Averting my eyes, I looked up to see a hairball I had coughed up a week previously and discreetly pushed under a rug. It had been attached to an invisible thread and was hanging from the ceiling, where it twirled in midair like a monstrous disco ball.

Dodging the legs of the guests, I ran out of the room and found 🐾 helping himself to a smoked salmon canapé in the lobby.

"But where are the paintings?" I spluttered with, I think, admirable understatement.

"Paintings? He's moved on from them," 🐾 mumbled through a mouthful of blini. "Canvases are so last year. He's all about installations now."

"But why didn't he just use your . . . installations? Why did he have to use mine?" I wailed.

"Something about creative renewal. Dunno, really. You know what these artists are like. Besides, I didn't really fancy it this time."

At this point our dialogue was interrupted by a scream, followed by a crash and then a collective gasp. Part of me wanted to run, but, unable to overcome my innate feline curiosity and believing (wrongly, as it turned out) that things couldn't get any worse, I slunk back into the exhibition room to see what had happened.

It appeared that one of the waitresses had been moving around the room, offering a tray of champagne flutes to the guests (who had no doubt realized that getting drunk was the best way to cope with the stench). However, the waitress had unwittingly strayed into the installation, whereupon she had placed a foot in mound number 3 of my "exploration of the human revulsion impulse." At this point the poor girl—possibly through embarrassment at having damaged the art, but more likely because she had experienced her own personal revulsion impulse—skidded, lost her balance, and sent her tray of glasses flying through the air so that they had landed, at great volume, among the nail-clipping petri dishes.

Meanwhile she executed some impressive (one might almost say feline) acrobatic maneuvers, before landing in a heap on shit mounds 4, 5, and 7.

As I skulked out through the lobby I heard her sobbing, "Next time you want me to work for an artist who deals in cat shit you'll need to bloody well pay me more money."

Honey, I thought, I couldn't have put it better myself.

CHAPTER 20

Bancy

> *Lots of people want to ride with you in the
> limo, but what you want is someone who will
> take the bus with you when the limo breaks
> down.*
>
> —Oprah Winfrey

I'm sure Princess would love to, but she'll be at a photo shoot for her new range of collars."

I was in the bedroom, listening to Helen talk on the phone in the living room, and sighed. Another job offer for one of the other cats. I was getting used to this; it was now early October and for weeks I had done nothing but lie listlessly around the flat, waiting for some work to come through. I had jumped to attention every time Helen's angry-cat ringtone had gone off, but it had never been an inquiry about me. Today, it seemed, was no different.

"I do have another female cat on my books at the moment," I heard Helen say, and my ears pricked up.

"She's no glamour puss, but she's available at short notice."

I rolled my eyes—charming!

"Pretty? Well, she's got a certain girl-next-door charm. Okay, great, I'll tell her to be ready for six p.m."

I headed into the living room, wondering what humiliation Helen had in store for me.

"Oh, there you are," she said. "I've got a booking for you. It's not a job, exactly, but it'll be good for your profile."

"Go on," I chirruped.

"It's the PAFTAs tomorrow night—the Pet Animals in Film and TV Awards. The Baron has been nominated for his latest commercial and needs an escort for the evening. His agent was hoping to book Princess, but she can't do it."

I pretended not to hear the last sentence.

"They'll send a car for you tomorrow at six," Helen continued, jotting the details down in her diary. "Try and smarten up a bit," she added. Then she reached for the cigarette packet, and I knew my briefing was over.

Last-minute substitute or not, this was proper A-list stuff: the PAFTAS were the biggest awards in the animal acting world.

I walked back to the bedroom in a daze. Princess was lying in her bed, flicking through a celebrity magazine.

"Princess, I'm going to the PAFTAs tomorrow."

"Good for you."

"I'm escorting someone called the Baron. Do you know who he is?"

She gave me an incredulous look and said, "Of course I do. Don't you?"

"Um, I'm not sure."

She flipped through her magazine, evidently searching for something, before pushing it across the floor toward me.

"That's the Baron."

On the page in front of me was an advertisement for Kit-e-Licious, featuring the orange-and-white tom whose face had filled my dreams for as long as I could remember. I stared at the page, openmouthed, as the room started to spin around me.

"His full name is Baron Romeo III, but everyone calls him

the Baron," Princess explained, mistaking my dumbstruck expression for ignorance.

"But, do you know him? How . . . I thought his identity was a secret," I spluttered.

"I've met him at parties a few times. It's no secret in the industry," she said nonchalantly.

"Well, what's he like?" I couldn't believe how blasé Princess was being.

"Talented. Ambitious. Word is he might be heading for Hollywood soon."

"Oh, my god," I said, looking at the advertisement again.

The Baron's face grinned at me from the page of the magazine. In just over twenty-four hours I would be escorting him to a star-studded awards ceremony! I was overcome by light-headedness and climbed into bed to lie down.

I began to wash, in a futile attempt to settle my nerves, but my mind was racing. There would be press in attendance at the ceremony, not to mention the great and the good of the show business world.

And I would be on the arm of one of the nominees!

My mind swam with possibilities. Was I, finally, on the cusp of proper, A-list stardom? If the Baron liked me, we could become *the* new celebrity couple—the cat world's answer to Brad and Angelina, or "Brangelina," as the press liked to call them. I wondered what our tabloid moniker would be. "Nanceo," perhaps. Or maybe just "Bancy."

"MIAOW," I said slowly, as I lay in bed. "Model . . . icon . . . actress . . . or . . ."

It had never occurred to me before, but maybe the "W" stood for "wife."

The following morning I woke with a start. I was afraid the whole thing had been a dream until I saw Princess's magazine lying on the floor, still open at the Kit-e-Licious advert. I stepped out of bed, walked over to my bowl, and started eating.

"Nancy!" Princess shouted from her bed. "*What* are you doing?"

"Er, eating breakfast," I replied sheepishly.

"Stop!" she shrieked. "You're attending the PAFTAs tonight. With the Baron. Do not. Eat. Anything."

I spat out my mouthful.

"Oh, right, sorry. Nothing at all?"

"Not if you want to look good for the paparazzi. If you're hungry, eat toilet paper. It's what they do in Hollywood."

"Toilet paper! Are you kidding?"

"No, Nancy, I'm deadly serious. This is your chance. Don't blow it."

My stomach was rumbling but I had to take Princess's advice: she knew the game far better than I did.

"Look," Princess said, her voice softening, "why don't you borrow one of my collars tonight? They're from my new range. It'll be good PR for me."

I glanced across at the bookcase where her collar collection was displayed, each one resting on a black velvet stand. I had never worn anything quite so glamorous. I picked up one made of pink satin.

"How about this?"

But Princess shook her head decisively. "Nope. Not for an awards ceremony. This is the right one for the job." She scooped up a collar covered in diamanté studs.

"Wow. It's very . . . bling. Do you think I can carry it off?"

"Nancy, you are escorting the Baron to the PAFTAs. You've got to look the part."

I slipped off my own frayed and faded collar and placed it on the bookcase, then Princess helped me to fasten its sparkly replacement.

"Perfect," she said, stepping back to assess me. She pushed her pedestal mirror in my direction.

I had to admit the collar looked good, although the nervous

expression on my face somewhat ruined the effect. I saw Princess in the reflection behind me, scrutinizing my appearance, and I smiled hopefully at her.

"You need to work on that smile," she said.

So I practiced smiling, looking backward coyly over my shoulder, and with my head tilted to the side. Frankly, I felt ridiculous, but Princess looked on encouragingly.

Helen swung the bedroom door open to tell Princess that the car had arrived to take her to the photo shoot, and soon I was alone in the bedroom, with just the mirror and my smile for company.

By late afternoon I was sick with nerves and hunger. I had spent a frustrating hour struggling with Princess's combs and brushes, trying to get my fur to do anything other than stick straight up, but nothing had worked. When Oscar and Gerald walked into the bedroom I asked what they thought of my "paparazzi smile."

"Just looks like your normal smile," Oscar commented unhelpfully.

At half past five I went and sat by the window in the living room to wait for the car, and at six o'clock exactly a stretch limousine pulled up outside Helen's flat.

"Oh, my god," I said. "That can't be for me."

Helen walked over to the window. "He's here. Come on, don't keep him waiting."

She went to the front door and held it open.

As I approached the car, a uniformed driver got out and opened the rear door, and I was hit by a smell of cologne so overpowering it made me gasp. I took a last lungful of fresh air before jumping in.

There, opposite me on the white leather seat, was Mr. Kit-e-Licious.

The Baron.

Mr. Big to my Carrie Bradshaw.

"Hi," I said, although for some reason the word came out in a high-pitched squeak. The Baron scrutinized me.

"Hello," he said, before adding, "you'll do," under his breath.

The limo pulled away from the curb, and I settled into the plush upholstery. I had never seen such a lavishly appointed car. The windows were blacked out, the lighting was ambient, and there was a minibar on one side, fully stocked with Kit-e-Licious snacks. I looked surreptitiously across at the Baron, who seemed deep in thought as he stared out the window. He was smaller in the flesh than he appeared in his commercials, but there was no disputing his good looks. His long fur was a deep shade of russet on his face and back, set off beautifully by his white chest and legs. His amber-green eyes were flecked with gold and his teeth were pristine white. I could see why he was destined for Hollywood.

"So," I ventured, this time my voice sounding about an octave deeper than normal. I cleared my throat. "I've never been to an awards ceremony before. I can't wait!"

He turned toward me with a look of surprise on his face, almost as if he had forgotten I was there.

"Really?" he asked, but before I could reply he had turned back to the window.

For God's sake, Nancy, just shut up before you say something really embarrassing, I thought.

So I looked out my window, too. Or rather, I looked at my reflection, taking the opportunity to practice my smile one last time.

As we drove into central London the traffic became heavier, and by the time we arrived in the West End the limo was moving at barely a crawl. The ceremony was being held at a smart hotel in Knightsbridge, and as the car passed Hyde Park Corner I could see a crowd of people gathered outside a grand-looking building.

"Just play it cool, Nancy," I said under my breath.

The driver maneuvered the limo into place around the corner from the hotel's entrance, and a porter opened our door. I jumped down to find that I was standing on a red carpet, and I could hear the noise of the excited crowd around the corner.

The Baron looked at me, and, for the first time that evening, he smiled. I noticed as he did so that the gold flecks in his eyes twinkled, and dimples appeared on his cheeks.

"Ready?" he asked.

"You bet!" I replied, activating my paparazzi smile.

"Make sure you stick with me," he said and I nodded.

I stepped alongside him and then we walked, shoulder to shoulder, along the red carpet toward the waiting crowd.

The sight of the crowd as we turned the corner made my heart lurch, and I was aware of my smile turning into a rictus grin. Some people had started screaming, "It's him!" and the line of cameras suddenly swung in our direction and began to flash. The Baron smiled broadly as he waved at the crowd. Some fans had thrown handfuls of Kit-e-Licious treats onto the red carpet, which he stopped to nibble on. Looking at the treats made my stomach rumble, but remembering Princess's strict instructions not to touch any food, I resisted. Instead I stood behind the Baron, trying not to look self-conscious.

Eventually, with a final wave, he turned his back on the crowd and we walked toward the steps at the hotel's entrance.

Here we stopped again, this time for the assembled press. To my surprise, I felt the Baron's head rub against mine in a gesture of playful affection. I looked at him in amazement, but his eyes were fixed on the cameras in front of us, which had exploded into flashes. I smiled at him, but before I could digest what had happened we were ushered inside.

The foyer of the hotel was packed with industry bigwigs, the animal nominees, and their escorts. Most of the award contenders were cats and dogs, but I also spotted a few rodents and birds in cages. I could hear laughter and the clinking of glasses, plus the odd yelp as a nominee's tail came into contact with a wayward stiletto heel. Groups of industry types stood in clusters: men in expensive suits and expertly groomed women.

I wanted to stop and take in the scene but the Baron kept

moving, so I followed at his heels, trying to dodge the legs of the humans. Once we had made it across the foyer we walked through a doorway into the hotel's ballroom, which had been turned into an auditorium for the night. A stage with a gold podium stood at one end, and the rest of the room was filled with rows of chairs.

An usher guided us to our seats in the front row. A few moments later a huge, shaggy-haired Old English sheepdog jumped onto the chair next to me. I smiled at him as he made himself comfortable on the seat, which wasn't easy given his size.

"Evening," he said gruffly.

"Hello," I replied. "What are you nominated for?"

"Best television commercial," he said, and I sensed the Baron's hackles rise on my other side.

"What's your commercial for?" I asked.

"Paint."

"Oh," I said, slightly nonplussed.

Just then a man in a tuxedo walked up to the podium, the lights dimmed, and a hush descended on the room. The ceremony was about to begin.

There were seemingly endless award categories to sit through, and I was aware of my stomach audibly gurgling as the evening wore on. I sensed impatience among animals and humans alike as we endured awards for "Best Rodent Choreography" (which went to a tap-dancing rat in a children's TV program) and "Best Synchronized Flying" (which was awarded, in absentia, to a flock of geese in a wildlife documentary). The Baron made little effort to disguise his boredom, tapping his paws impatiently on his chair. The sheepdog to my left had fallen asleep and was snoring with his head on my tail. A few seats down, a handsome Burmese cat licked his paws, not even watching the proceedings onstage.

Eventually the host announced the final award of the night, Best Animal in a TV Commercial: the Baron's category. I was aware of animals and humans stirring in their seats around me.

The lights dimmed and all eyes were on the screen at the back of the stage. The first nominee was the sheepdog, for De-luxe Emulsion paint.

In the commercial, he ran through a series of empty rooms, whose dull walls magically glowed with color as he passed through. The commercial ended to polite applause from the audience.

"No threat there," the Baron whispered to me.

Next up was the Burmese cat a few seats away, who fronted a campaign for Purrfect, a rival cat food brand. In his commer-cial he rubbed up against the ankles of a glamorous woman be-fore jumping onto a table and eating from a dish.

"Pah!" snorted the Baron dismissively.

I was amazed at his calm demeanor. He seemed so confident, so at ease. I wondered if I would be so laid-back if I were ever in his position.

"And our final nominee for the Best Animal in a TV Com-mercial Award is Baron Romeo III, for Kit-e-Licious," announced the host. The Baron's eyes were fixed on the screen ahead, but he gave no outward indication of nervousness.

A rousing orchestral soundtrack began to blare from the sound system. On-screen the Baron's face appeared in close-up, smiling enigmatically. The camera pulled back to reveal that he was in the driver's seat of a speedboat, on a moonlit lake. He thrust a lever forward and the boat zoomed out of sight, leaving an arc of foam in its wake.

Next, the screen cut to a beautiful female cat lying on a cush-ion in the turret room of a castle. She was gazing wistfully at the night sky through an open window. The sound of a helicopter emerged over the music, and the screen cut back to the Baron.

Now he was hanging by his front paws from the underside of a black helicopter that hovered above the ramparts of the castle. The music surged as the Baron released his grip and dropped onto the castle roof.

The female cat looked up, startled by the sound. She walked across her boudoir and jumped onto the windowsill.

Meanwhile, behind her, the Baron lowered himself into the room in a body harness attached to a suspension wire. In close-up, his paw placed a gold-colored pouch of Kit-e-Licious on her cushion. Just as the female cat turned around, the Baron pulled a cord on his harness and shot back up his wire, disappearing out of sight. The female cat looked around, suspicious, before walking cautiously toward her cushion. Seeing the pouch, she smiled. Then the Baron's face filled the screen once more, and he disappeared across the lake in his speedboat.

Over a close-up shot of the pouch, a husky voice intoned, "And all because the lady loves . . . Kit-e-Licious."

The lights in the auditorium came back up, and there was a tense silence as the presenter opened the gold envelope.

"And the award for Best Animal in a TV Commercial goes to . . . the Baron!"

The room erupted into cheers. I looked around at the ecstatic faces of the audience, and the Baron's wide grin as he soaked up the applause.

I was in awe!

As the Baron made his way up onto the stage to collect his trophy I started to clap and cheer. For a fleeting moment, I pretended that the adulation in the room was for me, that *I* was stepping up to the podium, ready to deliver a gracious and witty acceptance speech. I looked around at the whooping crowd, and the thought passed through my mind: "Next time, it'll be me!"

Once the Baron had returned to his seat clutching his trophy, the applause died down, and the audience began to file out of the auditorium.

What would be coming next? I wondered. A champagne reception? A VIP party at some exclusive members' club?

I followed the Baron as he made his way between the rows of seats. To my surprise, he headed straight to a side exit, which led to the waiting limo outside. Once we were in the car I looked at him and said, "That was amazing! Congratulations!"

"Thank you," he replied.

"So, where now?"

There was a flicker of embarrassment in his eyes. "Well, home, for you."

I was aware of a blush rising in my cheeks, and not wanting him to see how crestfallen I was, I turned to look out my window.

"Oh, of course," I said to the glass. I watched the Baron in the reflection as he yawned, stretched, then curled up on the leather seat.

In what seemed like no time at all the limo pulled up outside Helen's flat. The door opened and I turned to say good-bye, but I could tell from the way the Baron's whiskers were twitching that he was asleep.

"'Bye, then," I whispered before jumping down onto the pavement.

I watched the limo pull away, hoping to catch a glimpse of a paw waving at me through the rear window, but I saw nothing.

Standing in the chilly autumn air, my stomach rumbled again.

At least I can finally have something to eat, I thought.

I heard the front door buzz open, so I walked down the path and into the house.

CHAPTER 21

Nancy's Choice

*Home is not where you live, but where you
are understood.*

—Anonymous

The papers have arrived, Nancy."

It was the following morning, and Princess was standing next to my bed. I shook my head briskly, then followed her
into the living room, where Helen was sitting with the day's
newspapers spread out in front of her.

"Check this one out," Helen said, pushing one of the tabloids
toward me. It was open at the gossip page, and in the bottom
right-hand corner was a photo of the Baron and me on the red
carpet, his head nuzzling mine. His expression radiated cool
confidence; I was grinning from ear to ear.

The caption asked, "Who's that girl?" and the paragraph
underneath explained that the Kit-e-Licious star had been accompanied by a "mystery female cat" to the PAFTA awards.

"Could the famous feline lothario be about to settle down at
last?" it speculated.

"That's brilliant, Nancy, just what we wanted!" Helen exclaimed, but I could not share her enthusiasm.

I had spent the night unable to sleep, restlessly going over the
evening's events. As much as I had enjoyed the glamour and ex-

citement of the ceremony, I had felt an emptiness afterward, and not just because I hadn't eaten for twelve hours. I could not shake the feeling that the whole thing had been a sham. The Baron and I had not exchanged a dozen words all evening, and yet to see the coverage in the paper anyone would think we were an item.

Studying the photo, the truth finally dawned on me: I had not been on a date with the Baron; I had been a pawn in a strategy devised to generate publicity for him. He had needed a female cat to be photographed with, someone to get the press talking. He had wanted a glamour puss like Princess, but had made do with me.

Twenty-four hours ago I had thought my dream was about to come true, that I was on the brink of meeting my Mr. Right and becoming a celebrity. But instead I had discovered that the celebrity life was like Gerald's KittySlim food: it looked real from the outside, but tasted of nothing but cardboard.

"Oh, look, here's another one," Helen said, lifting a paper out of the pile to read aloud.

"'The Kit-e-Licious heartthrob was out on the town last night, attending the PAFTA awards ceremony. He was accompanied by a female cat identified only as Nancy.'" Helen glanced at me with a smile.

Then she looked back at the newspaper, and her smile faded.

"'He and his companion had parted company later in the evening, however, when he was spotted strutting his stuff with another tomcat at the Glitter Tray nightclub.'"

Helen paused as she looked over the article.

"Oh, dear. The Baron's people won't be very happy with that. But at least you were mentioned by name. That's the main thing."

I smiled ruefully. Helen should have volunteered Gerald or Oscar to be the Baron's escort. They might have been more to his liking.

I had heard enough.

I walked back to the bedroom and climbed into bed, feeling

utterly dejected. The Baron must have been laughing at me all evening, knowing that I was so starstruck by him that I would have done whatever he asked. All for the sake of a photo in a gossip column, designed to mislead the public about his romantic proclivities.

"*Bancy,*" I said bitterly.

How naïve I had been.

I drifted into a restless sleep and woke a short while later to find that Helen had gone out to a meeting. For the first time since moving to London I felt a longing to know what was going on in the life I'd left behind, so I logged on to Helen's computer.

There were dozens of e-mails in my in-box, mostly from Facebook friends asking what I was up to and why I had gone so quiet. I felt a pang of guilt upon seeing several e-mails from my owners asking me to get in touch. They had been annoyed with me at first, but their messages became more desperate in tone as the weeks had gone on. Continuing to scroll down the list, I stopped in my tracks when I saw an e-mail from Murphy.

Its subject heading was "MY bIRthdaY."

I smiled, remembering my own problems with the caps lock button when I had first learned to type.

HI nancy.

It's Murphy. How is London?

It's my birthday this weekend and I'm having a party at home. Please come if you can.

We all miss you. Brambles says do you need antibac wipes he will send them if you do.

Love Murphy

I checked the date, but the e-mail was over a month old; the party had been and gone. I had not even known it was Murphy's birthday. I felt a dull ache in the pit of my stomach and my eyes started to tingle. I read Murphy's e-mail again and couldn't stop the words forming in my mind: *I miss my home.*

I thought about the birthday party. I thought about my owners and the little people. I thought about Murphy struggling with the keyboard and mouse in order to e-mail me. I knew how much he hated computers, but he had persevered, determined to get an invitation to me somehow.

The tingling in my eyes was getting worse, and I quickly closed my e-mail account before the tears could come.

Hoping to distract myself, I opened Facebook.

My news feed was full of the usual mundane updates about my friends' lives. The humans moaned about work or the weather. Troy the show cat had posted photos of the latest addition to his trophy collection.

A few friends had posted a link to a new cat blog, which they said was the funniest thing they had read in ages. I felt a pang of jealousy as I remembered how people used to say the same about my blog, which I hadn't updated since I had moved to London almost six weeks ago.

The blog was called Cat Confidential, and I nearly fell off the desk when I saw that its author was Molly.

I could feel my heart pounding as I read some of her posts. The blog was a wryly observant account of life in a small town— *our* small town—in which she poked gentle fun at her human and feline neighbors. She was nothing if not prolific, blogging several times a week, sometimes even several times a day. The comments from her followers read "LOL! Molly, you rock!" and "Ha ha, Molly. Another hilarious post!"

How dare she? I fumed. Blogging was *my* thing. Molly had never even heard of a blog until I'd started mine, and she had shown nothing but disdain for it. Yet here she was, a few months later, blogging as if her life depended on it. And by the looks of it, with more followers than I'd ever had.

I closed Cat Confidential and stared at the computer screen, my tail twitching with annoyance. Then I jumped down from the desk and walked into the bedroom. Unusually, all three of my cat housemates were in the room.

Gerald was measuring out his prescription food into a bowl placed on kitchen scales. He carefully poured the dry food in, studying the digital display. He picked three biscuits out of the bowl then put two back in, his eyes still fixed on the tiny screen. He smiled, evidently satisfied, and placed the single leftover biscuit carefully back in the box. Then he began to eat the biscuits in his bowl one by one, making sure to chew each of them the requisite number of times before swallowing it.

On the other side of the room, Princess was trying on her collars. When she had fastened one around her neck, she would practice her facial expressions in the mirror, tilting her head coquettishly and placing her paw in front of her mouth with her lips slightly parted. Then she would return the collar to its stand and move on to the next one.

Oscar was working on his new act. He had spread some objects out in front of the window and was sitting next to a row of picture cards turned facedown. He stared intently at the back of a card before walking over to his collection of objects. With an expression of concentration he selected the roll of tape. Then he turned the card over, to reveal a picture of a ball of wool.

"Damn it!" he shouted, before returning the tape to its original position and taking another card. This time he purposefully selected the toy mouse, then turned the card over to reveal a picture of the tape. He emitted a strange growling noise through his gritted teeth.

"Oscar," I said after he failed to match the object to the picture for the sixth time in a row. "What am I about to do?"

"Er, dunno, Nance. Have a nap?"

"Wrong," I said. "Guess again."

Oscar scowled. "I never *guess*, Nancy. I'm psychic."

"Of course you are, Oscar," I replied.

Then I walked back into the living room and jumped up onto the desk. My Facebook page was still open on the computer.

In the status bar I typed, "Nancy . . . is coming home."

When I stepped off the train the following morning I was struck by the smell in the air. Rather than the exhaust fumes and smog of London, I could smell the autumn leaves on the trees, and berries on the hedgerows. I made my way up the hill from the station, listening to the birds in the sky above me.

"Isn't that *that* cat?"

"Which cat?"

"The one who killed six chickens onstage, of course!"

"Oh, my god, it is!"

Turning right at the corner shop, I trotted along the pavement toward NHQ but as I approached the driveway I stopped. I knew that my owners would have seen my Facebook status and would be expecting me, but I hesitated. Once inside it would be difficult to leave, and there was something else I had to do first.

I turned away from the house and padded along the pavement to the end of the street, where I turned right and headed up the hill toward Murphy and Molly's house.

All was quiet as I pushed my face through the cat flap. I slipped into the kitchen and looked around. The food bowls stood empty, and I could hear the kitchen clock ticking on the wall. Then I heard another noise, a tapping coming from the living room. It was a noise I knew well: the sound of typing on a computer keyboard. I crept over to the door and pushed it open a crack. Molly was sitting at a desk in the corner, with her back to me. I could see she was typing a new post in Cat Confidential.

"Oh, Murphy please don't put it on again; I'm trying to concentrate," she said without taking her eyes off the screen.

I peered around the door and saw Murphy sitting on the arm of the sofa next to the CD player.

"Just one more time, Molly, please. It's Nancy's song," he said before hitting play.

The familiar introduction to "Beautiful" by Christina Aguilera came through the speakers, and I could see Molly's head sink into her paws. Murphy's eyes were shut as he swayed from side to side to the music. He hummed the tune softly at first, but soon could not resist singing along, bravely attempting the higher-range notes in a voice that could politely be described as *falsetto*.

I saw Molly stuff her paws into her ears.

Murphy was singing at full throttle now, if not fully in tune. I stifled a giggle and crept into the room, where I sat on the floor in front of him, waiting for the song to finish. As the music faded I cleared my throat and said, "Hello, stranger."

Murphy's eyes sprang open and his jaw dropped. I was aware of Molly spinning around at her desk behind me.

"You should enter *Britain's Got Talent*, Murphy. You're exactly what that show needs."

His face broke into a smile. "Nancy! You're home!"

"Yes, I am," I answered, my eyes starting to tingle.

He jumped down from the sofa and walked toward me.

"You look . . . beautiful," he said, coyly.

"You don't look so bad yourself," I replied, and I meant it. He may not have had the Baron's dimples or beautiful coloring, but the affection in his eyes was worth more to me than anything the Baron had to offer. A look of concern flashed across his face as he asked, "Are you staying?"

I smiled at him.

"Yes, I'm staying."

As we made our way along the footpath toward NHQ, I asked Murphy if he wanted to come in to meet my owners.

"Not this time," he replied, "but I'll wait here for you."

I understood in that moment how long he had been doing

just that. Not only waiting for me to come home, but waiting for me to realize what he meant to me.

"Thanks," I said before padding down the garden path toward the house.

I heard one of the little people squeal with excitement as I poked my head through the cat flap, hastily followed by a "shh!" from one of my owners. I tiptoed out of the kitchen, across the hallway, and into the dining room, where I was greeted by a huge cheer from my owners and the little people. I noticed a homemade "Welcome Home" banner strung from the picture rail. I was pounced on by the little people and smothered in kisses, and in return I bit their noses playfully, like I had when I was a kitten.

When they finally put me down, I noticed Pip sitting in the doorway, trying his best to look disapproving, but with a trace of a smile on his lips. I walked up to him and said, "Hi, Pip. Did you miss me?"

"Hmmm," he replied noncommittally before turning his back on me and walking over to the food bowls.

It's good to be back, I thought.

Chapter 22

... Or Whatever

*Success is getting what you want; happiness
is wanting what you get.*

—Anonymous

Nancy's back fur good!" the local newspaper proclaimed
shortly after my return, and for a euphoric few days I felt
like an A-list celebrity in my own town. Everywhere I went a
crowd of well-wishers gathered to pat my head and tell me how
much I'd been missed. I may have been on the pavement outside
the corner shop rather than at the PAFTAs, but those heartfelt
expressions of affection were better than any award.

"Where are you off to next, Nancy?" people joked, but I
knew I would not be going anywhere. My compulsion to have
adventures had gone. I no longer felt the urge to follow strangers
home from the pub or to jump into a car if its door was left open.
"You're quite the homebody now, aren't you, Nancy?" my owner
commented one day as I lay sprawled out on the sofa, and I could
hear the relief in her voice. I suspect she missed the late-night
"taxi for Nancy" routine even less than I did.

I wanted to tell Murphy about the Baron, to reassure him
that, however the newspapers had depicted our "relationship," I
had found him vain, dishonest, and boring. I knew Murphy
would have seen the pictures of us at the PAFTAs, yet that night

was the one part of my London adventure he never asked me about. He loved to hear about my disastrous art exhibition and television commercial, and he laughed heartily at my stories of Helen and my cat housemates. But if I mentioned the PAFTAs his eyes glazed over and he would get distracted or change the subject.

I desperately wanted to explain that my night with the Baron had been the turning point for me, but somehow the opportunity never arose.

That was the way Murphy wanted it, and I had to respect his wishes.

What with people stopping me on the street, and the local newspapers sending photographers to the house, life was something of a whirlwind, and it was a while before I could check in with Team Nancy.

I was particularly keen to catch up with Brambles, worrying that his phobias and irritable bowel might have got the better of him in my absence.

Making my way across the back gardens one morning about a week after my return, I was relieved to see him sitting on his patio, enjoying the autumn sunshine. His delight at seeing me was evident.

"I heard you were back, but I couldn't quite believe it!" he said, a happy smile on his face.

"Well, I couldn't stay away from Team Nancy forever, could I?"

"Tell me all about it, then," he said, making himself comfortable.

So I told him about my London adventure and described my feline housemates. When I mentioned Gerald's Litter Kwitter seat he was, as expected, fascinated.

"I might have to get me one of those!" he exclaimed.

By the time I told him about my night at the PAFTAs his eyes were like saucers. While I talked I studied him closely, trying to gauge the mental state behind his happy facade. There was something different about him, but I couldn't put my finger on what it was. Suddenly it came to me and I stopped mid-sentence.

"Brambles! You're sitting on a crack in the paving!"

Brambles smiled shyly.

"I know. It's something I've been working on with my therapist. I've got rid of the antibac gel, too!"

It was my turn to listen in awe while Brambles explained that he had started seeing a pet psychiatrist, and together they were tackling his phobias and obsessive-compulsive behaviors. It was going to be a long process, his therapist said, but he was making excellent progress.

"Good for you, Brambles!"

"Go inside and check out my food bowl," he replied with a grin.

"Now, there's an offer a girl can't refuse!" I joked, heading into the kitchen.

There I found his food bowl on a mat dotted with spilled crunchies and covered in muddy paw prints—something that would have sent the pretherapy Brambles into a tailspin of anxiety.

"Wow, Brambles, that's amazing!" I said, and his smile spread from ear to ear.

"Thank you," he replied. "I couldn't have done it without Bella, though."

Bella, it seemed, had found her calling at long last. She had taken on Brambles as a project, a focus for her endless reserves of affection. Rather than sitting on her owners' front doorstep fretting that she was about to be abandoned, she spent her time with Brambles, patiently helping him to work through his OCD issues. In Brambles, Bella had found what she had always sought: someone who needed her as much as she needed him. Some might say they were codependent, but it worked for them.

Of course, Bella still welled up with tears when she saw that I was back, but I could see that they were tears of happiness, rather than tears of concern.

Number 29, I discovered, was still pursuing an itinerant lifestyle, sleeping in sheds and stealing food. It had been months since his escape and people had long since forgotten his fugitive status, but he continued to wear his eye patch, lest anyone recognize him and report him to the authorities. To be honest, I think he just preferred life that way: being answerable to no one was what he had spent his years of incarceration dreaming about. His friendship with Pip had also continued to blossom in my absence. I counted myself lucky if I got more than five words out of Pip on any given day, but he and Number 29 would chat for hours, finishing each other's sentences and laughing at private jokes.

The two of them often disappeared for hours on end, roaming the neighborhood like vagabonds. One night I saw them staggering home along the footpath, their skinny frames virtually indistinguishable from one another. I darted behind a tree so I could observe them unnoticed. Pip was wearing Number 29's patch and they were both giggling like schoolgirls. Number 29 was telling a story that Pip found so hilarious he could barely walk: it took them nearly half an hour to stagger up the verge to our back garden. Watching them from my hiding place I realized that, in all my time living with Pip, I had never seen him laugh. Number 29 brought out a side of Pip's personality that no one else got to see.

I resolved there and then that, one day, I'd get the two of them onto *Jerry Springer* for a DNA test.

If they're not related, I'll eat my collar.

My friendship with Molly pretty much picked up where it had left off, which is to say she tried her best not to be in the same room as me, and if she had no choice in the matter, she alternated between ignoring me and giving me withering looks.

I wanted to show I had no hard feelings about her blog, so I logged on to Cat Confidential and signed up as a follower. A few days later I noticed that she had done the same for my Mog Blog.

We never discussed what we had done, but I like to think it was our unspoken acknowledgment that the cat blogosphere was big enough for both of us.

My new, domesticated lifestyle meant that I had more time for my blog, and I was surprised to find that writing gave me far more pleasure than any of the other careers I had tried my hand at. Murphy was happy to sleep on the desk at NHQ while I tapped away at the computer, and in spite of the long break, the Mog Blog soon picked up new followers.

I worried that no one would want to read a blog written by a boring, "normal" cat; but Murphy reassured me, "If it's funny, people will read it," and, as usual, he was right. I discovered that there was just as much humor to be found in the minutiae of everyday life as there was in a tale of crazy capers.

As Murphy put it, "Crazy capers are *so* last year."

Making the final adjustments to a blog post one afternoon, it struck me that perhaps writing was the special talent I had been searching for; that maybe "writer" was what the "W" in MI-AOW had stood for all along.

And do you know the best thing about it? It was something I could do from home.

Acknowledgments

Apparently it's the done thing, at the end of a memoir, to acknowledge anyone who helped during the writing process. At least, that's what my editor says (I suspect she's hoping for a mention). I guess it's the book equivalent to an Oscars acceptance speech, only without the emotional breakdown and horrific evening wear.

Much as it goes against my feline nature to show gratitude to anyone of the human persuasion, I suppose there are a few who have helped me to get where I am today. You could call them my *other* Team Nancy.

So, here goes.

To my wonderful agent Diane Banks, for not dismissing outright what must have been the worst book pitch in history, and for championing me every step of the way since (even though I've always had a sneaking suspicion you don't actually *like* cats!).

To my editor Becca Hunt, for your enthusiasm and professionalism, and for "getting" my sense of humor. Mostly.

To my owners (big and little), for being my chauffeurs, publicists, playmates, and caterers. I did well to choose you.

To all the cats featured in the book (and their owners) for

your cooperation, and to the people of Harpenden for welcoming me into your homes and ensuring I always return home safely.

And to my original Facebook gang (you know who you are), for giving me the idea to write this book in the first place.